London Survey'd

Dad

Happy Birthday

fun & joy

Malcolm

ROYAL
COMMISSION
ON THE HISTORICAL
MONUMENTS
OF ENGLAND

London Survey'd

THE WORK OF THE SURVEY OF LONDON 1894–1994

Hermione Hobhouse

ROYAL COMMISSION ON THE HISTORICAL MONUMENTS OF ENGLAND

Published by the Royal Commission on the Historical Monuments of England,
National Monuments Record Centre, Kemble Drive, Swindon SN2 2GZ

© RCHME Crown copyright 1994

First published 1994

ISBN 1 873592 19 1

British Library Cataloguing in Publication Data
A CIP catalogue record for this book is available from the British Library

Designed by Chuck Goodwin, 27 Artesian Road, London W2 5DA

Printed in Great Britain by The Print Factory, Unit 2, 24 Thames Road, Barking, Essex 1G11 0HZ

Contents

London Survey'd:

THE WORK OF THE SURVEY OF LONDON 1894–1994

Illustrations

Commissioners

Chairman's Foreword

This book, and the exhibition at the Museum of London to which it relates, together mark the centenary of a London institution – the Survey of London.

The Survey began as the personal initiative of a single individual, the architect C R Ashbee, backed by a committee of fellow enthusiasts, and it became a project supported by the London County Council (LCC). The LCC and its successor body, the Greater London Council (GLC), saw the Survey's register as a necessary tool for preserving London's wealth of historic buildings. Since 1986, the Survey has been part of the Royal Commission on the Historical Monuments of England (RCHME), the national body responsible for recording and disseminating information on the country's architectural and archaeological heritage.

The founders of the Survey of London were both public-spirited and far-sighted, since their initiative, like many private campaigns, foreshadowed action later taken by government. It started as an attempt to create a list of buildings of historic and architectural importance in London, with the intention of preventing their accidental or thoughtless destruction, an aim in which it was supported by the London County Council. From this developed the series of volumes on the buildings of London, researched and written on a parish basis, which are familiar to so many. So far, over forty parish volumes and seventeen monographs on single buildings have been produced, and two very substantial volumes on Poplar and the Isle of Dogs will be published later this year.

The centenary exhibition has been generously supported by a number of other London bodies, notably the Museum of London and the Guildhall Library, the London Division of English Heritage and other institutions and individuals whose help is acknowledged elsewhere. The book has been written by Hermione Hobhouse, who retires this year, but, as can be said of all Survey of London publications, it is a project to which all members of the team have contributed. Hermione Hobhouse has been General Editor of the Survey for eleven years. We are grateful to her for her notable contribution to the Survey's long history.

PARK OF MONMOUTH

Acknowledgements

The appearance of this book and the exhibition to which it relates is due to the support of the Royal Commission on the Historical Monuments of England, which has been responsible for the work of the Survey of London since 1986. I am particularly indebted to those Commissioners – Bridget Cherry, Derek Keene and Anne Riches – who read the text and commented on it.

The staff of the Museum of London have been very helpful throughout, as have those of the Greater London Record Office and Photographic Library, English Heritage and the City of London Art Gallery and Guildhall Library, all of whom have allowed us to reproduce material from their archives. Gayne Wells, the Chairman of the London Society, generously gave me access to the Society's archives. Illustrations have also been provided by the Art Workers' Guild, the Chelsea Conservative and Unionist Association and the National Portrait Gallery.

I have also received help from a number of private individuals including Miss Felicity Ashbee, Alan Crawford, Nicholas Meinertzhagen, and Cecil Farthing, former Director of the National Buildings Record, and above all from Mrs Millicent Godfrey. As the guardian of the Godfrey Archive, she gave me the run of the magnificent collection of letters, minutes and ephemera put together by W H Godfrey, which records the doings of the London Survey Committee between 1910 and 1939. Without these, this book would have been a very dry record.

In researching and writing this book, I have received assistance from colleagues within the Royal Commission. John Bold read the text and provided advice and help for both book and exhibition. Many of the drawings reproduced and the archive photographs come from the National Monuments Record, and my thanks are due to Stephen Croad, Tony Rumsey and their colleagues for help in locating them; the modern photographs were taken by Derek Kendall. Kate Owen and her colleagues have been responsible for the production of both the book and the exhibition.

My major debt is to my colleagues on the Survey of London, past and present, for their contribution to the maintenance of this great enterprise and for their help and advice to me personally. I must express my gratitude to Francis Sheppard, my predecessor as General Editor, and to John Greenacombe, present Deputy Editor, for reading and commenting on the text. Peter Bezodis, Victor Belcher and Andrew Saint have also contributed to my knowledge of the history and practices of the Survey, as has Ashley Barker, formerly Surveyor of Historic Buildings to the Greater London Council. Finally, I must express particular thanks to Tara Draper, research assistant on the illustrations for both book and exhibition.

Hermione Hobhouse

INTRODUCTION

The Survey of London is a remarkable institution, a historic buildings project which has endured for a hundred years, enlisting wide-ranging support during that time from private individuals, local government bodies and the Civil Service. As Sir Osbert Lancaster observed in 1973, 'When I am tempted to think ill of the GLC, a temptation to which I am, from time to time, subject, I think of the Survey of London and hold my peace. No other public body . . . supports so magnificent a publication.'[1]

Though the Survey is today best known for its scholarly volumes – 'a series which aims at describing the buildings and other objects of architectural and historical interest in London, parish by parish, and of recording the history of each parish'[2] – it was founded not as a publishing venture, but as an attempt to create a 'register' or list of buildings of historical and architectural significance. This initiative was taken in the 1890s, at a time when the historic fabric of London was seen to be under threat, and the cataloguing of the capital's architectural and historic buildings was intended to identify them so clearly that the danger of destruction would be eliminated.

The notion of a register or 'list' developed rapidly into a fuller account of the monuments of each parish; even by the 1920s some account of the development of the built fabric was being given. When in the 1940s, under the post-war legislation, the statutory lists came into being, both providing the catalogue of significant buildings, and at the same time giving them government protection, the Survey of London was sufficiently well established to survive as a publication. The great London historian T F Reddaway could describe a volume as a 'storehouse of information clearly and interestingly set out', adding that 'good documentation and excellent illustrations enhance a well-presented book'.[3]

This opinion was so widely held that, when, in 1986, the Greater London Council (GLC) was abolished, the Survey of London, together with its sister department, the Historic Buildings Division, survived. The Survey was given a new home in a non-departmental public body, the Royal Commission on the Historical Monuments of England (RCHME), while the Historic Buildings Division of the Architect's Department became part of English Heritage. This was entirely appropriate, since, for reasons set out in this book, there is a historic sympathy between the aims of the Survey and those of the Royal Commission, and the men who shaped their early years worked closely together. Though both the Royal Commission and the Survey have become well known subsequently for their skills in recording and classifying buildings, it should be remembered that both bodies were set up to produce registers or lists of buildings of national importance; they are, therefore, part of the initiatives taken to give Great Britain better and more effective ways of conserving the national heritage.

1 *Sir John Lubbock, Chairman of the London County Council 1890–2*

Some late Victorian and Edwardian statesmen were involved in this endeavour, one of the most notable names being that of Sir John Lubbock MP (1834–1913) [1], author of the 1882 Ancient Monuments Act. In general, however, government action in preserving historic buildings was little and ineffectual, and the credit for action must go to private individuals. These worked to found the London Survey Committee, and similar organisations – the Society for the Protection of Ancient Buildings (SPAB), the London Topographical Society (LTS), the National Trust, even the London Society. Much of their work consisted in mobilising public opinion, and in promoting preservation schemes, later taken over by government at local and national level. This pressure ultimately brought into being the town planning acts of the 1930s and the post-war listed building legislation.

This year – 1994 – the Survey of London celebrates one hundred years of service to London buildings, and it is a suitable moment to record its achievements. It can fairly claim, in the words of Percy Lovell, a former Secretary of the London Survey Committee, to have 'won a recognised and permanent position as the recorder of all that is interesting in London topography'.[4] It is, however, a story that must be read at several levels. It covers the actual work of the individuals on the London Survey Committee in recording and writing about groups of buildings, the compiling of the 'register' of London buildings fit to be conserved, and the saving of buildings under threat. It also covers the creation of a prototype for action, first at metropolitan, and then at national level, in the listing and recording, and the preservation, of buildings of architectural and historic interest and importance.

LONDON UNDER THREAT IN THE 1890s

The London Survey Committee, or, as it was known until 1914,[5] the Committee for the Survey of the Memorials of Greater London, was founded by the Arts and Crafts architect C R Ashbee (1863–1942) and a group of sympathetic colleagues in the early summer of 1894. This was because of the threat to a particular local landmark, but also in response to a growing feeling of unease about the demolition and destruction of historic buildings in London. This was a general feeling, which concerned a number of Londoners. In the words of E W Riley, Architect to the London County Council (LCC), in a 1903 report: 'London is now being more rapidly altered than at any time during the last century, and many historical houses and objects of archaeological interest are being destroyed without any record being made of them. In some cases the owners are quite unaware of the interest attaching to the buildings . . .'.[6]

This report only reflected what many antiquarians and historians of the metropolis had known for a quarter of a century. Those years had seen great

2 *The Oxford Arms Inn, demolished in 1875, recorded for the Society for Photographing the Relics of Old London*

changes and 'improvements' in London, including the loss of pre-Fire half-timbered buildings and the elimination of many obsolescent building types – galleried inns, the substantial dwelling houses of City merchants, both within the square mile and in former villages outside, almshouses, and even some Wren churches.

Great Britain lagged behind other European countries in its official protection of historic buildings. France had had an elaborate system administered by the Comité Special des Arts et Monuments since 1837, while the Kingdom of Bavaria had established a historic buildings inventory in 1887, published as the *Kunstdenkmaler von Bayern*.[7] Though the 1882 Ancient Monuments Act had established the principle of control over what today we call the 'national heritage', it covered only uninhabitable monuments like Stonehenge, and, as far as destruction went, an Englishman's home was truly 'his castle'.

A number of individuals and organisations had endeavoured to tackle the problem before Ashbee. In 1875 the Society for Photographing the Relics of Old London had been established by Alfred Marks and like-minded friends. The intention had been to record the Oxford Arms Inn, an outstanding half-timbered galleried inn threatened with demolition [2], which epitomised the losses going on in London. The project proved so popular, however, that a further one hundred

*3 Queen's Head Inn, Southwark,
from an engraving by T R Way*

photographs of threatened or demolished buildings were issued over the next eleven years.[8]

In 1880 the Topographical Society of London was founded, counting among its early members the London historians Henry B Wheatley (1838–1917) and Cornelius Walford, Major-General J Baillie, one of the promoters, and Laurence Gomme (1858–1916), a London historian, later to become a notable London local government officer. Its primary purpose was the publication of maps and other historic documents, 'a series of the greatest value in the elucidation of the history of London'. However, another part of the Society's work was seen as 'registering the various changes that are continually taking place in London . . . a task . . . of the greatest importance', for which no organisation existed. Two members had been recording the recent excavations at Leadenhall, and other demolished buildings. The Society discussed the setting-up of local committees, it being agreed that the 'system of registration of changes' was 'of too vast a character for one or two persons to deal with adequately'. Interestingly enough, the report of the meeting recorded the discussion of the proper type of division, whether like 'the City, the East End, Southwark, Westminster, Marylebone . . . or in accordance with the postal divisions'.[9] This is the sort of problem which perplexes all urban historians choosing a manageable compass for their work, and still taxes the managers of the Survey of London from time to time. This ambitious start faltered and the Society was re-founded as the London Topographical Society in 1896. Throughout its existence, the LTS has had a number of links with the London Survey Committee, both through a shared objective in making aspects of London history more widely known and in common membership.

This increasing concern about the disappearance of London landmarks and even major monuments was reflected in publications as well as in the work of the various pressure groups. A number of books recording lost buildings appeared in the next few years, including *Vanishing London* by Roland Paul, published in 1894, and the *Reliques of Old London* series, using T R Way's lithographs with text by H B Wheatley, mourning the changes [**3**]. To these can be added the splendid series of water-colours commissioned by Sir Charles Chadwyck-Healey from John Crowther in

4 *Wych Street, the Strand, in 1901, painted by Philip Norman. This street was obliterated for the making of the Aldwych*

the 1880s and 1890s, now in the Guildhall Library, and Philip Norman's *London Vanished and Vanishing* of 1905 [**4**]. As Norman put it, 'Growth and destruction have gone hand in hand, and soon perhaps it will be as difficult to find an old house within the four-mile radius as to light upon an unrestored church.'[10]

THE FOUNDATION OF
THE LONDON SURVEY COMMITTEE

5 *C R Ashbee, photograph by Frank Lloyd Wright*

C R Ashbee [**5**] was a successful architect and designer who put his socialist principles to work in setting up not only an architect's office, but also the Guild of Handicraft, a band of craftsmen who lived communally and worked on designs for furniture and jewellery. In the 1890s the Guild was based at Essex House, 401 Mile End Road, Ashbee's home and office in the East End [**6**].

The particular disaster which led Ashbee to form the Committee for the Survey of the Memorials of Greater London was a *bêtise* on the part of the London School Board, which had demolished a fine hunting lodge, built c 1600, in Bromley-by-Bow to provide a site for a Board School [**7**]. However, as Alan Crawford, Ashbee's biographer, has pointed out, it was difficult for the School Board to recognise the 'palace' behind 4 and 6 St Leonard Street, Bromley-by-Bow, with its curtailed corner towers and later sash windows.[11] The Board had already sold the materials to the house-breaker, and though, in some embarrassment, the Board recovered the panelling and ceiling of the State Room for the South Kensington (now the Victoria & Albert) Museum,[12] the damage was done. As Ashbee wrote bitterly later:

We now have on the site of King James' Palace a well-built Board School . . . sanitary, solid, grey, grim, and commonplace. What we might have had with a little thought and no extra expense would have been an ideal Board School with a record of every period of English history from the time of Henry VIII . . . as a daily object lesson for the little citizens of Bromley.[13]

Ashbee appealed widely for help in setting up a 'watch committee' to compile a register, writing a circular setting out his aims and speaking at a meeting at the Architectural Association in March 1894 to arouse interest. The Survey Committee met first on 25 June 1894, at Essex House. In addition to Ashbee himself and Ernest Godman (d 1906), who became the first Secretary, ten other members were present, all but one classed as 'active' members – that is, they would be expected to carry out the work of the Committee. Sir Frederick Leighton was persuaded to become President, the architect E W Mountford Vice-President, and Walter Besant, the London historian, promised his support.

The subjects discussed and the conservationist approach adopted at that first meeting have a familiar ring. The main work was that of compiling a 'register' of important buildings, which would alert Londoners to their importance, and

6 *Essex House, Mile End Road,*
c 1890, where Ashbee founded the
Committee for the Survey of the
Memorials of Greater London

7 *The Old Palace, Bromley-by-Bow,*
whose demolition in 1894 provoked
Ashbee to found the London Survey
Committee; drawn by Ernest
Godman, Secretary of the Committee

prevent their destruction. As will be described, these registers later came to be published as the 'parish volumes'. In addition, the committee was to compile an 'emergency list' of buildings in danger, which were to be recorded both as a matter of urgency, and also to be campaigned for; later on the members showed a concern over heavy-handed or destructive restoration.

The idea of monographs on 'particularly interesting buildings which it might be difficult to do full justice to in the Register' was raised at this first meeting. The list included a number of studies ultimately published, including those on the 'Palace' itself, in Bromley-by-Bow, the Trinity Hospital in the Mile End Road, and Eastbury House, Barking.[14]

The early members of the Watch Committee were, in Crawford's words, 'a mixed bunch'; they met later in the year at a 'Watch Night Supper' to get to know each other better. The original group included A P Wire, a teacher and local historian, who contributed a number of photographs, Harry Lowerison, another local schoolteacher and journalist, a number of architects, including Cecil Brewer, of the well-known architectural partnership of Smith and Brewer, A E Nutter, another draughtsman in Ashbee's office, and Francis R Taylor (1864–1948). These names and many others can be traced through the lists of the Active Committee printed at the beginning of all volumes published until the LCC took over the Survey of London in 1952.

The amateur nature of the early work is underlined by the need to invite the Architectural Association Camera Club to visit Eastbury House and Parsloes Hall, Dagenham, both in Essex, in order to obtain photographs. Photography always presented problems in the early years, and the Committee was much indebted to active members who were competent photographers, many of whom were responsible for developing and printing their own films. Edward Yates (d 1957), for instance, a member of an old-established City firm dealing in timber and other building materials, and who later became an officer on the Committee, undertook a lot of photographic work for the Survey of London, and also some independent commissions for individual members, in particular for W H Godfrey.[15] His correspondence reveals the difficulties presented by the need to get buildings photographed, and the technical problems of developing and printing the results.

The first meeting of the Committee opened with some £59 in hand, but the members agreed to club together to buy a hand lithographic press, at a cost of between £40 and £50, on which to print the monographs.

Despite its apparent amateurishness, the Committee for the Survey of the Memorials of Greater London set its members a clear series of objectives in carrying out the surveys of buildings, whether the results were to be published as a single monograph or as part of the parish series. At the first meeting (25 June 1894, adjourned to 2 July) the divisions of the survey areas had been discussed.

LEASEHOLDERS. LENGTH OF LEASE.	LOCAL PUBLIC BODIES.	DATE OF WORKS. (DIFFERENT PERIODS UNDER VARIOUS HEADINGS.)

The house was destroyed in January 1894. + a new gin-palace occupies its site. bearing still the name of the old one

The main part of the structure was of wooden construction. It consisted of ground, 1st. and other floors. + had also a basement whose floor was level, at the back of the house with the surface of the garden.

At the back. + running up the ground + first floors was a

8 *Survey form recording 'The Spotted Dog' in Poplar High Street*

Because of the position of Essex House, the area to be covered was taken as twenty miles from Aldgate pump, both northward and eastward into rural Essex, with the Thames as the southern boundary, an area split into twenty-six districts, later subdivided, with each district allotted to one or more researchers.[16] For the purposes of publication the traditional parish seems to have been taken as the unit, and this was later set out more clearly by the Joint Publishing Committee (*see* Appendix 2). There were printed forms to be filled in, some of which have survived [**8**]. The information sought came closer to that required by local authorities than by architectural historians: ground landlord; leaseholders; length of lease; local public bodies; date of works (different periods under different headings); condition of repair; historical notes; bibliography, references to books; other notes, 'for Watch committee (but not necessarily for publication)'.[17]

These details provided a picture of the individual buildings or monuments being recorded, and researchers supplemented the information gleaned from 'Parson, Postman and Policeman'[18] with sketches, photographs and the occasional measured drawing. The objective was a catalogue of notable monuments and buildings, clearly identified, which could be used by both amateur and local authority. Considerable emphasis was placed on the voluntary nature of the work, though the Committee was well aware of the need for professional expertise. In advice to other local groups who wanted to embark on such a project, it was stressed that the 'superintendence of the work' should be in the hands of an

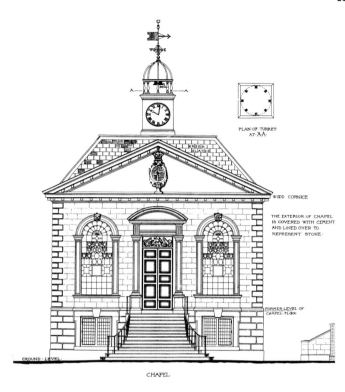

PLAN·OF·TURRET
AT·A·A·

KITCHEN
ELEVATION

WOOD CORNICE

THE EXTERIOR OF CHAPEL
IS COVERED WITH CEMENT
AND LINED OVER TO
REPRESENT STONE·

FORMER·LEVEL·OF
CHAPEL·FLOOR·

GROUND·LEVEL·

CHAPEL

THE TRINITY HOSPITAL IN · ·
MILE END: AN OBJECT LESSON
IN NATIONAL HISTORY, BY · ·
C. R. ASHBEE, M.A., ARCHITECT.

*BEING THE FIRST MONO-
GRAPH OF THE COM-
MITTEE FOR THE SURVEY
OF THE MEMORIALS OF
GREATER LONDON.*

*PUBLISHED BY THE
GUILD & SCHOOL
OF HANDICRAFT,
ESSEX HOUSE, BOW,
LONDON, E. 1896.*

9 *The Trinity Hospital, Mile End
Road. Elevation of the chapel
drawn by Ernest Godman for the
first monograph*

10 *Title page to* The Trinity
Hospital in Mile End, *the first
monograph published by the
Survey Committee*

architect, or 'a man versed in antiquarian work, who is within reach of expert architectural advice'.[19]

By 1895 much information and material had been collected, without, as yet, the means to publish the results. Ashbee had put forward the idea of a 'Chelsea Committee' to continue the work in the west, but a more immediate distraction was the threat to the Trinity Hospital in the Mile End Road, a group of almshouses, built for retired employees of Trinity House, which the Corporation wished to sell for redevelopment. It became the subject of the first Survey of London monograph, *The Trinity Hospital in Mile End* (1896) [**9**, **10**]. This publication set the high standard of book production which has always characterised the Survey publications. The campaign for the building was also successful politically. The furore stirred up by Ashbee, and the support obtained from public figures, from Gladstone to William Morris, ensured the survival of the building.

The role of the London County Council

More important in establishing the register of 'old and interesting buildings' was the growing connection with the London County Council. The Council came into being in 1889, in that period of enthusiasm for civic improvement which occurred at the end of the 19th century, stimulated by the example of Paris and of Germany, possibly inspired by the growing recognition of London as the heart of an Empire. It is difficult today to conceive of the euphoria which led Londoners of all classes to look forward with optimism to a new age, but it is worth recalling the civic ambition which found the creation of a metropolitan authority a matter for pride. In the words of an early LCC Alderman:

> the truth that London is essentially a community of human beings which ought to have an organic government of its own, was established . . . It may seem strange to the upper ten thousand who live in the pleasantest parts of the town . . . that the shopkeeper or the artisan may have his imagination fired with the greatness of London and with the idea of making all its parts work together for the good of the whole.[20]

11 *Sir Laurence Gomme, Clerk to the London County Council 1900–15*

The involvement of the London County Council in the work of saving London buildings appears to have been largely due to the personal interest of the writer and historian Laurence Gomme [**11**]. Gomme, recruited as Statistical Officer to the Council, and Clerk from 1900 to 1915, was a very considerable historian in his own right, who seems to have been responsible, in fact as well as in name, for carrying out many of the Council's initiatives in the field of activities known as Records and Museums. He published two substantial works on London, but had wider interests in medieval villages, and in folklore, being founder of the Folk-lore Society. Amongst his legacies to London are the names of 'Kingsway' and 'the Aldwych', names based on his knowledge of the earlier topography of the area.[21] His support, both official and personal, for the Survey project seems to have been important in developing the idea of a register, as in the other areas in which the LCC was concerned with historical matters. Though there were a number of liberal-minded and well-disposed members of the Council, the support of such a senior member of staff was critical in dealing with a highly organised bureaucracy.

12 *No. 17 Fleet Street, photographed in 1884. This half-timbered building with later additions was purchased by the London County Council in 1900*

The actual involvement of the LCC in the listing of buildings was, however, initiated by Sir John Lubbock, Chairman of the LCC in 1890–2. Lubbock was a remarkable polymath; originally a banker and responsible for the Act bringing in Bank Holidays, he was also an authority on ants, and an avid botanist. His is a notable name in the early history of historic buildings preservation in this country: as a Liberal MP, he was the author of the 1882 Ancient Monuments Act, for which he battled for over five years.[22]

Early in 1896, he suggested that the LCC's General Purposes Committee should be asked to advise the Council on the right course of action 'in the case of the contemplated destruction of any building of historic or architectural interest'. This was followed at the end of the year by a Conference of Learned Societies, to which the Survey Committee sent Ashbee as its representative.

This conference, held on 4 December 1896, at which both the Society for the

13 *No. 17 Fleet Street in 1906, after restoration by the London County Council*

Protection of Ancient Buildings and the newly formed National Trust were represented, signified the LCC's commitment to the preservation of buildings and monuments in its area. Ashbee reported on the work of the Survey Committee in compiling a register, which was commended by the conference, and a proposal was put forward that it should be extended to the whole LCC area. The following year the Council agreed to print the register in conjunction with the Committee. At the same time, it took steps to increase its own powers in the matter of historic buildings. It obtained powers to expend money from the rates to save buildings, the first beneficiary being No.17 Fleet Street [**12**, **13**]; in 1901 it took over from the Royal Society of Arts its scheme for marking the former homes of prominent citizens, which became the 'Blue Plaque Scheme'. Accounts of the houses so honoured were issued in penny leaflets by the Council, later issued as *Indications of Houses of Historical Interest in London*.[23]

It is worth looking at the results of this conference, which set out the pattern for the preservation of so much of London's threatened heritage. In February 1897 the LCC's General Purposes Committee reported on the four resolutions passed at the meeting. The first of these laid down the desirability of the making of a 'register or list of buildings of historic or architectural interest in London . . . such . . . as to admit of amplification, both as to buildings and as to details of buildings'. To carry it out, the formation of a 'general committee of representations of the different societies' was proposed, something the Council was not minded to endorse. However, the work of the Survey Committee in the East End was commended, and it was proposed that it should be extended to the rest of London, 'it being understood that such registers are formed for the use' of the LCC; finally, the conference asked that the General Purposes Committee should consider printing the 'register from time to time with suitable drawings and illustrations'.[24] This last recommendation led in due course to the printing by the Council of part of the material prepared by Ashbee's colleagues on the Committee, as the first volume of the register in 1900. It also stimulated the efforts of the LCC's own endeavours through the work of the Local Government, Records and Museums Committee.

In his report of May 1897 to the Survey Committee, Ashbee described the results of the conference with appreciation. By this time, the membership of the Committee was divided into 'honorary' members, who received a copy of the volumes in return for their subscriptions, and 'active' members, who carried out the recording and writing work. Ashbee went on to describe the methods used by the latter, and claimed that the first volume, 'containing the record of some six or eight parishes', was almost complete in manuscript, together with illustrations. He announced that the Committee would turn its attention to Chelsea. He also listed some eight proposed monographs, which included those on the Old Palace and the Great House at Leyton, eventually published, and others on Aldgate and Essex House which never appeared (*see* Appendix 1). Twenty 'special cases' had been noted, in some of which the Committee and its allies had been successful, including the Trinity Hospital and Stratford-atte-Bow Church, threatened by road-widening.[25]

The first publications

Despite these successes in saving buildings, there were delays in the production of the first volume of the register. This publication, entitled *The Survey of London . . . the first volume of the Register*, dealt with one parish only, that of Bromley-by-Bow. It did not appear until 1900, when it was published with the support of the LCC, and thereafter the name 'Survey of London' seems to have been adopted instead of 'register'.[26] It established a format for the parish volumes which was only gradually altered: a map of the parish or area covered, an introduction setting out the particular problems or characteristics of the volume, a list of the monuments, and at the end the measured drawings, photographs and sketches which illustrated them. The descriptions of the buildings are supplemented by historical notes and by bibliographical references. Gomme contributed a preface which described the conference held in 1896 (inexplicably and confusingly misdated as 1897), which led directly to the LCC agreeing to pay for the publication of the volume. Ashbee provided an introduction:

> In laying before the citizens of London the first volume of a work that may, perhaps, never be finished, but that at least seeks to mark down the main lines on which her great history could be preserved and studied, it will not, perhaps, be out of place to say a few words as to the origin of the present volume.[27]

He started by describing the organisation and methods of the team which created the record, and then, deploring the losses in Bromley-by-Bow during the period, rehearsed the losses, both in London and on the outskirts, since the Committee had been at work. In characteristic fashion, he then put forward his ideals for the betterment of London and its citizens.

However, despite the welcome appearance of the first parish volume, the Survey Committee faced a crisis: there had been no meetings or reports since 1897. But in June 1900 an important meeting was held in Chelsea, chaired by the Liberal MP Leonard Courtney (1850–1918) and attended by a number of distinguished figures, including Lord Monkswell, Chairman of the LCC 1903–4, Laurence Gomme, Lord Justice Sir John Rigby, and Lord Balcarres, later President of the Survey Committee. It was perhaps symbolic that the meeting was held in Chelsea, the subject of the next parish volume, and the home of so many of the more artistic and conservationist-minded members of the establishment.[28] Sir Ernest Meinertzhagen [14], a much-travelled barrister with a house in Cheyne Walk, was recruited to the Committee. An 'intensely religious man, rigidly conservative in politics, yet in some ways as open-minded in spirit as he was open-handed in his actions', his interests in the LCC included working-class housing as well as historic

14 *Sir Ernest Meinertzhagen, Hon Treasurer of the London Survey Committee 1907–33*

15 *The 'Essex House pink', which was found growing at Essex House. This design by C R Ashbee was used as a symbol of the Guild of Handicraft*

buildings. As Honorary Treasurer of the Committee from 1907 until his death in 1933, and also LCC member for Chelsea 1910–33, he was to provide a vital link with the LCC.[29] The following year, research on the parish of Chelsea began, the work being entrusted to the newly recruited W H Godfrey (1881–1961). Thereafter, the Committee turned its attention to Chelsea.

However, a good deal of recording did take place, and a number of monographs on individual buildings, some threatened and some saved, appeared (*see* Appendix 1). From the first they were seen as a useful method of directing attention to a building, whether in the nature of an appeal, like *The Trinity Hospital in Mile End* (1896), or as an obituary, like *The Old Palace of Bromley-by-Bow* (1902). The monographs were by different authors, sometimes by a number of hands, but they were all elegantly produced and illustrated by original drawings. Several were printed at the Guild of Handicraft, and their covers bear the characteristic Essex House pink, designed by Ashbee [**15**]. Like other early volumes, they have brown paper covers, intended for fastidious library owners who wished to have the volumes bound to suit themselves. (Some 'subscribers' continued to insist, even into the 1970s, on their volumes being delivered unbound and untrimmed to facilitate binding.) The earlier volumes are illustrated by sketches and measured drawings rather than by photographs, and some even have hand-coloured heraldic achievements – the Trinity Hospital monograph has a hand-coloured drawing by Godman. Though some are extremely slight, depending on the subject and the author, they often record buildings since disappeared.

Two great houses threatened by apparent obsolescence and decay were the subjects of *The Great House, Leyton* (1903), and *Brooke House, Hackney* (1904), then in use as an asylum. Ironically, the latter was saved from the house-breakers but badly damaged by a bomb in 1940. Before the remains were cleared away in 1954–5, further research and some excavation was carried out, being published in

1960 as Volume XXVIII of the Survey of London, and the two volumes provide an interesting contrast in method and approach.

Two monographs were contributed by Ernest Godman, that on *The Old Palace of Bromley-by-Bow* (1902), which expanded the account in Volume I, and one on *The Church of St. Dunstan, Stepney* (1905), which had recently been damaged by fire. He also wrote up his notes on Essex, collected for the Survey Committee but technically outside its boundaries, and these appeared in 1906 as *Norman Architecture of Essex* and *Medieval Architecture of Essex.*

In 1902 Ashbee moved with the Guild of Handicraft to Chipping Campden, in Gloucestershire, and, though he did not sever his connection with the Survey of London, inevitably he had less time and energy for its work. Ernest Godman's illness and death, early in 1906, made new management essential. Fortunately, a remarkable triumvirate was available to take over, men who were to exemplify Drake's saying that it is not in the undertaking but in the carrying-through that any great endeavour should be judged.

This is not, however, to belittle Ashbee's contribution in founding the Survey Committee and in having the perception to see the need for a 'register' – today's 'statutory List of Buildings of Special Architectural and Historic Interest' – which would enable people to recognise the importance and significance of historic buildings. One can perhaps wonder at the naïvety, or perhaps the expectation of higher standards in public life, which assumed that developers and owners would not demolish buildings once they *knew* them to be of historic importance, without any legal compulsion. Under Ashbee's leadership the Committee built up a considerable collection of material – by 1906 some 2,500 drawings, photographs and measured drawings.[30] He also carried the not inconsiderable financial burden of the deficit in the Committee's expenses, due to the gap between subscriptions and the everyday expenses of carrying on the investigation and of bringing out the early monograph volumes, for which the Committee was still indebted to him in the 1920s.[31] He was no preservationist for the sake of preservation; historic buildings were for him only part of the ideal city. In his preface to Volume I of the Survey of London, Ashbee provides an Edwardian view of that elusive ideal – the quality of life – in the way that he links the preservation of historic buildings to the provision of museums and of parks and open spaces. He summarised the task before 'all citizens of London':

> *we plead that the object of the work we have before us, is to make nobler and more humanly enjoyable the life of the great city whose existing record we seek to mark down; to preserve of it for her children and those yet to come whatever is best in her past or fairest in her present . . . and to stimulate amongst her citizens that historic and social conscience which to all great communities is their most sacred possession.[32]*

NEW MANAGEMENT
FOR THE SURVEY OF LONDON

A meeting held at Lord Monkswell's house in Chelsea on 8 March 1907 confirmed the new arrangements, appointing Sir Ernest Meinertzhagen Honorary Treasurer. The three men who were to shape the Survey of London for the next quarter of a century were all members of the Active Committee in 1907. Philip Norman (1842–1931) [**16**] became Chairman, and then also Editor; Percy Lovell [**17**], an architect in private practice, was recruited as 'a keen and energetic successor' to Godman; W H Godfrey [**18**] was active in recording and writing the volumes, though he did not become Honorary Assistant Editor until 1921.

Philip Norman was already an established authority on old London buildings, and known as an accomplished water-colour artist who had recorded a large number of threatened buildings. He came from a long-established City banking family, his father being George Warde Norman of Bromley Common, Kent, Governor of the Bank of England. Through his family, Norman had important contacts both with the City and the LCC. One nephew, Montagu Norman (later Lord Norman) (1871–1950), was the almost legendary first professional Governor of the Bank of England, and another, Ronald Collet Norman (1873–1963), was Chairman of the LCC in 1918–19. Originally intended for the sherry trade, Philip Norman returned from Jerez to England to the Slade School in 1882, and thereafter dedicated his life to the study of old buildings. His *London Vanished*

16 *Philip Norman,*
Chairman and Hon Editor
of the London Survey
Committee 1907–31

17 *Percy Lovell, Secretary of*
the London Survey
Committee 1907–39

18 *Walter H Godfrey, member*
and later Hon Editor of the
London Survey Committee
1907–52

and *Vanishing* was illustrated with seventy-five of his own water-colours, sixty of them of demolished buildings [**19**; *see also* **4** and **21**]. He was Chairman and Editor of the Survey Committee from 1907 until his death, contributing the text to two monographs, a vice-president of the Society of Antiquaries, an early member of the LTS, of the SPAB, and the Art Workers' Guild. A W Clapham remembered him as a 'personality . . . with a gracious figure and a very gracious mind, his manner had a touch of aristocratic aloofness, which . . . rather enhanced the courtesy and kindness which lay behind'.[33]

Percy Lovell was Secretary of the Committee until 1939, with the exception of the war years, when he was serving with the Northumberland Fusiliers. He emerges as a likeable if idiosyncratic figure: educated at Marlborough and Trinity College, Cambridge, he was articled to Aston Webb. His office in Great Smith Street, where regular monthly meetings were held, became the focus of the Committee's activities. He was an excellent draughtsman, contributing both text

19 *Old Inn Yard behind Harpur's Arms, Holborn, painted by Philip Norman*

and drawings to the volumes, and provided a sense of urgency and order to the work which had not perhaps been apparent earlier. He wrote several Survey publications, and it is perhaps significant that after his death the Survey Committee was effectively wound up. He seems never to have married, living with a maiden aunt of whom he appears to have been very fond, fastidious about not deserting her at weekends unless she had some entertainment laid on. In 1913 he was appointed first Secretary of the London Society, of which Aston Webb was first Chairman. His work for the London Society was virtually full time and complemented his work for the Survey Committee, and he ran both organisations with great success until 1939. He made the Society an important force in interesting Londoners in town planning and other matters, displaying considerable managerial and social skills. He organised outings, visits and lectures from prominent speakers and politicians on town planning issues affecting London, and he published a monthly journal which is an important source of information about the preservationist battles of the period. The Society's concerns extended to the proposed demolition of important buildings, and Lovell's contacts strengthened his and Godfrey's campaigns for threatened buildings.[34]

The third in this triumvirate was Walter Hindes Godfrey, another architect, for whom work for the Survey was only part of a wider campaign. He was trained in the former office of George Devey, whose moribund practice he rebuilt with the help of his partner, Edmund Wratten. He worked at Sudeley and Herstmonceux Castles and at the Temple Church, and was architect to Beverley Minster, and Chelsea Old Church, which he rebuilt after the Second World War. His list of publications is impressive, and reveals the breadth of his interests. He started with a life of Devey, and continued initially with London subjects, often as Survey of London publications, putting his knowledge of individual buildings to good use, as in his *History of Architecture in London* (1911). After a move to Lewes he contributed extensively to the knowledge of local Sussex buildings, without abandoning his interest in London. He was active in forming the Graphic Records Committee in 1931, and became a founding member of the staff of the National Buildings Record (NBR) in 1941, one of the most lasting projects to owe its inception to the Second World War, now also part of the RCHME. He was its first Director from 1941 until 1960.[35]

In many ways Godfrey was typical of the literary architects, also trained in the understanding and repair of old buildings, who have had such an influence on the development of the Survey. In 1944 he published *Our Building Inheritance*, on the impending post-war threats to historic buildings. His intention was 'to prove that good building, apart from its claim on our regard as a work of art, is never incapable of adaptation to the right sphere of usefulness in perpetuity, and that it is sheer waste to pull down a fine structure on the pretext that a change of purpose has rendered it obsolete'.[36]

In 1907 the Survey Committee faced problems in getting the work carried on. It could not afford to publish the volumes out of the slender subscriptions and a number of the earlier publications remained unsold.

It had published a number of monographs and there had been some successes in saving buildings. The monograph *Crosby Place* (published in 1908), by Philip Norman and the architect W D Caröe, reflects one such partial success, though it is not entirely clear who can claim the credit for even that degree of preservation.

Crosby Place, later Crosby Hall

Even in the 1890s Crosby Place had been an icon for preservationists concerned about the City [20]. It was a great 15th-century City merchant's hall, erected by the wool magnate Sir John Crosby in the 1460s. It stood behind the frontage on the east side of Bishopsgate and was probably originally a complex of courts, of which the Hall was only a part. On Crosby's death in 1475 it passed briefly to Richard, Duke of Gloucester, and continued to enjoy considerable importance as

20 *'Remains of Old London in 1894', a popular chromolithograph by Arthur C Payne, showing St Ethelburga's Church, St Helen the Great and Crosby Hall*

Remains of Old London in 1894.
Sketched by Arthur C. Payne.

the home of a number of City notables until the end of the 16th century. In the 1520s it was occupied briefly by Sir Thomas More, whose son-in-law William Roper was tenant in 1547. It escaped the Fire of London, but came down in the world socially. Crosby Place was divided up into several tenements, and the Hall itself was divided laterally, becoming first a Presbyterian meeting-house, then a warehouse. When it was advertised in 1831, it was rescued and restored by a

21 *Interior view of Crosby Hall under demolition, from a water-colour by Philip Norman* c *1907*

Mrs Maria Hackett. By 1868 it had become the banqueting room of a City restaurant, but in 1907 the site was bought by the Chartered Bank of India, Australia and China for redevelopment. A powerful group, including Norman and Godfrey, Nigel Bond of the National Trust, Gomme and Clement Y Sturge from the LCC, and even the City Corporation, was unable either to persuade the Bank to change its intentions, or to provide enough money to purchase Crosby Hall. Gomme contrasted this with the way public opinion treated such matters when they happened on the Continent: 'Were it St. Mark's at Venice [where the campanile had recently collapsed] or a piece of Swiss scenery about to be cut through by a railway, the British Public would be up in arms and we should have no end of protestation.'[37]

A monograph had already been planned on the building, and the Chartered Bank, though refusing to budge from its original intention, provided facilities for recording and even numbering the stones and timbers of the Hall [21].

At this moment the Edinburgh town planner Patrick Geddes intervened: he already had an interest in land in Chelsea, as part of his scheme for self-governing halls of residence for the reorganised London University. By 1907 the Chelsea scheme – More Hall, as it was to be called – had the backing of Ashbee, Lethaby, Gomme and H G Wells. Geddes seems to have seen the idea of transferring Sir Thomas More's City residence to his Chelsea home as a way of increasing support for the flagging More Hall scheme. He sent a telegram to Godfrey, asking whether he could re-erect Crosby Hall in Chelsea; the answer was yes! In three years the salvaged parts of the Hall, essentially the magnificent timber ceiling and the stonework of the interior of the hall and of the oriel window, were reinstated on the Chelsea Embankment [22] – a reconstruction that owed much to Godfrey's skill and reticence as an architect. The scheme had important repercussions for the Survey Committee, in that relations with the LCC were much improved through the collaboration between Godfrey and Sturge over the project.[38]

22 *Crosby Hall from the Chelsea Embankment after removal and reconstruction in 1907–10*

Negotiations with the LCC

Though the LCC had paid for the printing of Volume I in 1900, relations between the Committee and the Council seem to have cooled – perhaps, as Andrew Saint has suggested, because of Ashbee's intransigence in his dealings as a would-be Chelsea developer with the LCC.[39] No formal relationship between the LCC and the Survey Committee existed, despite the fact that the Clerk, Laurence Gomme, seems always to have been on good personal terms with the Survey Committee (not least, perhaps, because his son Austin had worked in Ashbee's office[40]).

The reasons for this crisis are several, and reflect not only Ashbee's declining influence, but possibly also a power struggle within the LCC, where there could have been a feeling that this sort of register was more a matter for local government than for voluntary effort. Not all LCC members were convinced of the need to preserve buildings, and the Architect and the Clerk, between whose departments a historic rivalry developed, were both interested in the work of the Historical Records Committee. In October 1903 a report to this Committee, by E W Riley (1852–1937), Architect 1899–1919, put forward a scheme for the continuation by his department 'of the survey of London begun by "The Committee for the Survey of the Memorials of Greater London"'. He proposed the division of London into fifty-eight districts, not all of which he opined would fill a volume by themselves. He suggested a trial period of six months during which two assistants who had 'special training for this work' would 'survey buildings about to be demolished . . . examine and report upon objects of interest found in excavation during rebuilding' and carry out a historical and archaeological survey of a particular district of London. He suggested that his department should ask for the co-operation of the Survey Committee and of the relevant local authorities in each district, and that he should be empowered to seek 'gratuitous private assistance'. This report was approved, with the instruction to concentrate on the Aldwych and Kingsway (covered in due course in Volumes III and V) and the parish of St John, Westminster, then the subject of 'improvement'.[41]

In the event, though the LCC did not bring out a volume in competition, the Survey Committee had to finance the second volume of the register – *The Parish of Chelsea (Part I)*, in 1909 – from its own resources. However, good relations with the Council were finally secured through the support of Clement Young Sturge, LCC Member for Westminster 1904–11, because of his interest in the reconstruction of Crosby Hall. As a Municipal Reformer, and a member of the majority party after 1907, he was in a position to 'command Sir Laurence Gomme's interest' and advance the work of the Survey. Sturge was a somewhat eccentric figure, described by Godfrey, who designed an Italian garden for him in Rodborough Heights, Stroud, as 'immensely corpulent'. He always travelled from Gloucestershire 'with two large cats in baskets, which he liberated in the railway carriage'.[42]

The agreement with the LCC

In 1909 the Committee was invited to enter into negotiation with the LCC, for a joint venture in creating a register, it having been agreed, in Gomme's words, that 'it was desirable that a register should be made of buildings of historic or architectural interest in London'.[43] By this agreement, finally achieved after prolonged negotiation and dated 25 July 1910, the Survey of London publication programme was to be managed. The preamble acknowledged that both Survey Committee and Council had been compiling a register and collecting material on buildings, and that duplication should be avoided. Under this agreement, renewable every five years and remaining substantially in force until 1952, the Committee agreed to deposit all its original material for past or future volumes with the Council, subject to its availability for consultation. The printing of future volumes was to be paid for by the Council; some volumes, up to a maximum of 250, were to be issued *gratis* to members of the Survey Committee who had paid their guinea subscription or worked on the volumes – a provision which caused problems whenever the Council had a fit of penny-pinching. Volume I was to be the prototype for the series, and future monographs were not to trespass on any area not yet covered by a parish volume. The management was to rest with a Joint Publishing Committee, something on which the Committee had insisted, but where the Council was to have a majority.[44]

This arrangement put the relationship between Council and Survey on a formal footing – not easy where one party, though wealthy, was bound by the restrictions of local government management and finance, and the other was entirely dependent on the enthusiasm and resources of volunteers. This relationship was much assisted by Meinertzhagen's chairmanship of the Committee until his death in 1933, and the tacit support of the officers of the Council for the project. Though Gomme retired in the middle of the First World War, and died shortly afterwards, a member of his Department, W W Braines (1872–c 1945), was responsible for the research and production of the alternate Council volumes in the parish series, from the outset until his retirement in 1935.[45] It was Braines who set the very high standard of scholarship in documentary research which distinguished the Council volumes, a tradition which was carried on by his immediate successor in the post, Ida Darlington (1905–70). As it became clear that no privately supported group could compete in quality with a metropolitan body like the LCC, assistance was given on occasion in both documentary research, and even in the production of drawings.

The Survey Committee representatives on the seven-man Publishing Committee were initially Norman, Lovell and Godfrey. On Norman's death in 1931, Godfrey became Honorary Editor, and H W Fincham (c 1860–1952), a stationer and box manufacturer from Clerkenwell, who had devoted forty years to the library and museum of the Priory of St John, was recruited to the Publishing Committee.[46] The Committee was in abeyance during both wars, but after the Second World War J W Bloe replaced Lovell.

The Council representatives tended to change with political fortunes. Thus in 1914, under Meinertzhagen's chairmanship, the members were R W Granville-Smith, Sturge's successor in Westminster, and (Sir) Andrew Taylor (Hampstead), both Municipal Reformers (otherwise Conservatives), and W C Johnson, a prominent Liberal who sat for Whitechapel. In 1933, after Meinertzhagen's death and the Labour victory, the members still included two Conservatives, Alfred C (later Lord) Bossom (1881–1965), an English architect turned successful American developer who none the less sat as an LCC alderman,[47] and A McD Gordon, who represented Stoke Newington. But the Chairmanship went to J H MacDonnell, Labour member for Southwark, who survived on the Committee as an adviser until after 1952. MacDonnell, himself a collector of Londoniana, who lent material for Survey volumes, was a *bête-noire* of Lovell, who found the change from the supportive Meinertzhagen a trial.

THE JOINT PUBLISHING COMMITTEE, 1910–1939

From the signing of the agreement in 1910, the London Survey Committee worked in double harness with the LCC on the Joint Publishing Committee, more or less amicably, though with differing approaches and a different end product. During this period the Joint Publishing Committee produced Volumes III to XXIV of the parish volumes, or the 'register' (to use Ashbee's original phrase). This arrangement offered the Survey Committee the opportunity of producing regular publications and seeing the work of the Survey of London carried forward, but exposed it from time to time to the changes of direction and financial crises to which all democratic bodies are prone.

The Survey Committee functioned very much as a group over these years, meeting monthly to plan the publication of volumes and action on other matters. It was held together by Percy Lovell as Secretary, and the Committee functioned from his office, first in Great Smith Street, and then, around 1914, at No. 27 Abingdon Street, which became the official address of both the Survey Committee and the London Society. In 1929 both societies moved to Lancaster House, then the home of the London Museum [**23**]. A lively correspondence between Lovell and Godfrey (PWL and WHG) has survived from the later years, after Godfrey had moved out of London. It was Lovell who organised the traditional Watch Night supper for the fortieth anniversary of the foundation of the Committee, on 14

May 1934. It was held at Pagani's Restaurant in Little Portland Street – an informal dinner, 'not more than 22 or 23', morning dress not black tie, tickets to cost 7s 6d, to cover food and tips, but not liquid refreshment.[48]

Before reviewing the subjects of these volumes, and analysing the different approaches of Committee and Council, it is worth looking at two other aspects of the Survey Committee's work during this period – the monograph volumes and the work of preserving buildings threatened with demolition: all three topics appeared regularly on the weekly agendas.

While all three, Norman, Lovell and Godfrey, were involved with writing both monograph and parish volumes, the two great protagonists for threatened buildings were Lovell and Godfrey. After the former became Secretary of the London Society in 1913, soon after its foundation, he ran both organisations – not so much in tandem as a pair – with great success till 1939. It was a very convenient arrangement since the London Society's concerns, though primarily with town planning matters like roads, appropriate development and zoning, also covered demolition of important buildings. This community of interest was recognised very early, as Lovell reported in 1913: 'It was felt that [the Survey Committee's] special sphere of labour largely covered the Antiquarian side of the . . . Society's work . . . It is part of our policy to hand over matters of antiquarian interest that come to our notice to be dealt with by this body.'[49]

But there were other concerns for the London Society – of which roads and good communications were one of the most important. There was no hard and fast divide, as Ashbee's remark quoted earlier shows, between the conservationists and the town planners. In this endeavour, architects played a full part, and Lovell ran a conservationist body of considerable 'clout' until 1939.

Campaigns for buildings under threat

The list of buildings threatened with demolition over which Lovell and Godfrey intervened on behalf of the London Survey Committee is long, and includes almost every major 'case' in London between 1907 and the outbreak of war in 1939. Perhaps the term needs some definition, since Lovell and Godfrey were usually faced with the total demolition of a building with little or no statutory

LONDON LAUGHS . . . By LEE

LONDON SURVEY COMMITTEE

"What I really want, old chap, is a large-scale map showing where the pretty girls cluster thickest."

23 'London Survey Committee', a cartoon by 'Lee' of the London Evening News. This commemorates not only an unorthodox view of the work of the London Survey Committee, but also the Committee's offices at Lancaster House, then the home of the London Museum

protection; their objective was to prevent its destruction, but this could normally only be done either by raising sufficient money to purchase the building outright *and* find an alternative use, or, occasionally, by shaming a wealthy owner or institution into abandoning his plans. The mere recording of a building before its demolition came a poor second in their scheme of things. The 'recording of threatened buildings' as carried out today, when a building is recorded in anticipation of properly sanctioned partial or complete demolition under a statutory provision, did not exist. The scale of loss throughout the period was, of course, very great. Though the supply of old inns and half-timbered buildings had dried up, the 1920s were to see the loss of most of the remaining great family mansions in the West End, more demolition of City churches, the destruction of Waterloo Bridge, and the rebuilding of virtually the whole of Regent Street.

The Survey Committee had always concerned itself about threatened buildings from its earliest days. One category which concerned it was that of groups of institutional buildings where well-meaning trustees were selling off sites in central London in order to house their pensioners more comfortably in the country. Outstanding cases of this sort had been Christ's Hospital, in which 'the Committee had taken a continuous and active interest', taking the view that 'its destruction will be among

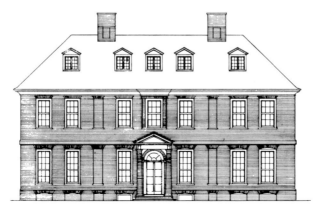

24 *Battersea House, north-west elevation, a measured drawing for the London Society* c *1936*

NORTH WEST ELEVATION

the worst and most short-sighted cases of vandalism in the last 50 years',[50] and the Foundling Hospital, both demolished. However, as has been said, Trinity Hospital in the Mile End Road had been saved, as was Morden College, Blackheath, also the subject of a monograph. Bromley College, London Road, Bromley, another 17th-century almshouse, was threatened by a road-widening scheme, which was fiercely and effectively contested by Lovell and Godfrey in 1938.[51]

Sometimes it was only a last-ditch effort, as when Lovell wrote to Godfrey in February 1932: 'Could you try a letter to the "Times" as Chairman of the Survey Committee praying for Waterloo Bridge? I gather the matter is to be more or less settled on Tuesday, so Powys [Secretary of the SPAB] tells me and we are trying to get a last despairing wail!'[52]

25 *St John's Institute, Hackney, now Sutton House, in 1929*

In other cases, 'with the firm of WHG and PWL at the helm',[53] the Committee was very effective. They were active in the case of Terrace House, Battersea, part of St John's College and threatened by a large public housing scheme, eventually saved because Arthur Greenwood, Minister of Health, was persuaded to use recent legislation to put a preservation order on it; appropriate tenants, Mr and Mrs Stirling, were installed, together with their Pre-Raphaelite collection, in what is today known as Old Battersea House [**24**].[54]

In the case of St John's Institute in Hackney, now Sutton House [**25**], which F C Varley drew for the Survey Committee in the 1890s, Lovell played a key role. In 1936 the Rector found he could no longer afford to maintain the building, but Lovell was able to persuade the National Trust to take it on, though he had to organise much of the campaign and to raise money from charitable trusts and private donors. As he wrote to D Matheson, Secretary to the Trust from 1934 until

1945: 'The real fact is that I am the only person who is really trying to find the money. If others would peg away too we should get it. Cannot some of your influential folk put in a word for us with the Pilgrim or similar Trust?'[55]

In the event the money was raised, over £1,000 of the purchase price of £3,000 being due to Lovell's efforts.

Monographs

The monographs, or studies of a single building, vary considerably in quality and substance (a complete list is given in Appendix 1). From the first, they were seen as a useful method of directing attention to a building, whether in the nature of an appeal, like *Trinity Hospital* or *Eastbury Manor House, Barking*, or as an obituary, like *The Old Palace of Bromley-by-Bow*. Occasionally, like that on *Swakeleys, Ickenham*, they partake of the triumphal. They were a convenient way to attract attention to a building, and to promote the work of the Committee. The volumes, as was suggested at the time, also provided a convenient sop for subscribers when the supply of 'parish volumes' faltered. In the early years they were printed at the Guild of Handicraft, either at Essex House or in Chipping Campden, and the quality of their production set a high standard for all subsequent volumes.

Under the agreement with the LCC, only the Survey Committee had any interest in the monographs, but it precluded the publishing of a monograph on a building in an area for which a parish volume had not appeared, except with the prior assent of the Publishing Committee. The minutes and correspondence of the Committee show that several monographs were projected, usually on buildings threatened with destruction, but never undertaken, while two Chelsea volumes – those on the old parish church, Volume VII (1921), and on the Royal Hospital, Volume XI (1927) – were originally projected as monographs, and should more properly be so. Subjects proposed included Kew and Eltham Palaces, and Boston Manor, Chiswick, at that time in Middlesex, and the threatened Church of All Hallows, Lombard Street, in the City.[56]

The subjects of some projected monographs, such as the Foundling Hospital, were covered by others.[57] Lovell had fought hard to save the Hospital buildings when it became clear that the Governors had decided to abandon their historic site in Bloomsbury, and rebuild outside London, commenting to Godfrey: 'The Governors are practically non-existent except in name; the real Governor is Nichols the Secretary. He has, with a friend, collected all the material for years past for a 3-vol. book on the Hospital.'[58] Despite his disappointment, Lovell was able to help Nichols in his recording of the doomed buildings, commenting two years later that the 'photographs of the Hospital and fittings and pictures are the finest I have ever seen . . . the whole place has been measured from floor to ceiling . . . the

material is, of course, far in advance of anything that has been done for any [LCC or LSC] volume'.[59] In due course the material was made available for Volume XXIV [**26**]. Ironically, after most of the buildings had gone, Lord Rothermere was persuaded to buy a large part of the site for public use.

Lovell welcomed volumes on other subjects from outside organisations, such as *The Queen's House, Greenwich* (1937), largely based on existing research, offered to Godfrey by George Chettle (d 1960), a former partner of Ashbee, and Inspector of Ancient Monuments, who had worked on the house for the Ministry of Works.[60] It was funded by Sir James Caird (1864–1954), a wealthy shipowner who had financed and endowed the National Maritime Museum.[61] In Lovell's words:

> *Collaboration of this nature is very welcome to us, for we are a hard working band of enthusiasts who receive little encouragement in our efforts to record the important vestiges of old London and its surroundings . . . There is, I think, a definite advantage in having monographs on our public buildings in a standard format with the imprint of the London Survey, and I have hoped that we might manage to build up a valuable series in this way.[62]*

26 *The Foundling Hospital chapel, famous for its connection with Handel*

SWAKELEYS, ICKENHAM.

SECTION THROUGH STAIRCASE HALL.

Swakeleys, Ickenham [**27**] celebrated a successful campaign to save the building in which Lovell and Godfrey were involved. The Carolean house was 'threatened with destruction in the welter of a newly developed building estate'[63] in 1923, when the whole estate was sold to Messrs Cross & Stedman. Fortunately the house, garden and outbuildings [**28**] were bought by Humphrey John Talbot, a public-spirited individual, who consulted the SPAB about a permanent future for them. Godfrey was able to use his friendship with the Herbert family, whom he had known for nearly twenty years, to provide the house with a more secure future. The Hon Mervyn Herbert (1882–1929), third son of the Fourth Earl of Carnarvon, a British diplomat with a well-connected American wife, persuaded the Foreign Office Sports Association to take part of the building for their headquarters.[64]

27 *The fine Carolean house at Swakeleys, Ickenham, was recorded by the London Survey Committee in 1932. Section through the staircase measured and drawn by A F Lodge*

28 *Swakeleys, plans and sections of the dovecot and icehouse, measured and drawn by A F Lodge*

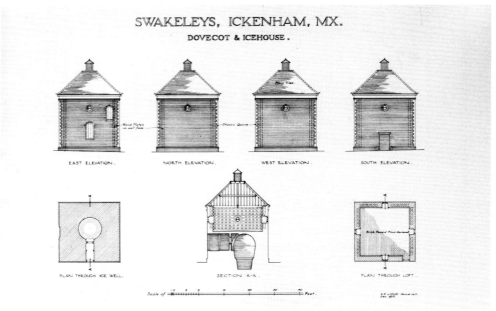

SWAKELEYS, ICKENHAM, MX.

DOVECOT & ICEHOUSE.

EAST ELEVATION.   NORTH ELEVATION.   WEST ELEVATION.   SOUTH ELEVATION.

PLAN THROUGH ICE WELL.   SECTION A–A.   PLAN THROUGH LOFT.

Parish volumes

Between 1912 and 1952 twenty-two volumes were produced alternately, in equal numbers, by Council and Committee (see Appendix 1). These were originally intended as the publication of the register or list of monuments in each parish or area. Inevitably, however, an element of explanation and historical interpretation of the whole fabric of the area began to develop, and an increasingly divergent approach to content and emphasis of the volumes appeared quite early in the series. Nevertheless, the partnership of Council and Committee endured for over thirty years, largely because of the diplomacy and personal skills of the people operating the system. All the volumes were published by the Joint Publishing Committee under the nominal joint editorship of the Clerk to the LCC and the Honorary Editor to the Committee, and usually appeared alternately from the two sets of authors. The names of subscribers and of the Active Committee appear in all volumes, even those from the Council. The Committee volumes – although often the work of several hands – also bear the name of an author from the Active Committee, of whom Godfrey was the most constant. He wrote all four Chelsea volumes (Vols II, IV, VII and XI), contributed to Volume VI on Hammersmith, wrote Volumes XXI and XXIV on St Pancras with Marcham, and was involved in providing drawings for others. He also wrote two monographs – *Swakeleys, Ickenham* (1933) and *The Church of St. Bride, Fleet St* (1944) – and worked on a third, *The College of Arms, Queen Victoria Street* (1963).[65]

The choice of areas to be covered by the Council was more carefully made, and on the whole more thoroughly carried out. The credit for the text of the Council volumes was given to those responsible; from the first, Volume III, *The Parish of St. Giles-in-the-Fields (Part I)* (1912), Laurence Gomme paid tribute to the research skills of W W Braines of the Records, Publications and Museums Section of his Department. Braines joined the LCC in 1892, and appears to have been early recruited to the work on historic buildings. In 1910 he took on the research for the Council volumes, and seems to have been very largely responsible for increasing the range and standard of research and for bringing new sources into the field. Many of these hitherto unrecognised sources were taken over by the LCC, on occasion rescued not only from oblivion but also from physical decay. To well-known aids to historical research, such as poor-rate records, were added those of the various Commissions of Sewers, and the Middlesex Deeds Registry, actually acquired by the Council in 1935. Braines retired as LCC Librarian in 1935, to be succeeded by Ida Darlington, who served as Archivist and Librarian from 1935 to 1967.

Ida Darlington joined the LCC as a historical research assistant in 1926, and started work on the Survey of London. She succeeded Braines on the Survey and

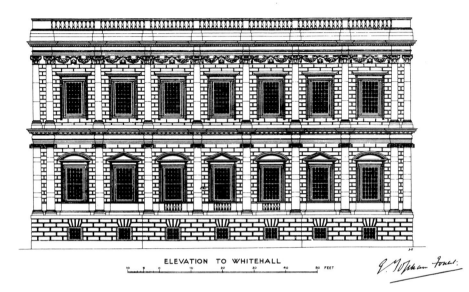

THE BANQUETING HOUSE WHITEHALL

ELEVATION TO WHITEHALL

29 *The Banqueting House,*
Whitehall, measured and drawn for
the London County Council

in the Members' Library, and was, one suspects, an able colleague from the start in the matter of sources.[66]

Braines, and, in due course, Darlington, were responsible for an impressive series of volumes. This series started with the St Giles's volumes (Vols III and V), approved by the Council in 1903 because of the threat to Lincoln's Inn Fields from the redevelopment scheme for the making of Kingsway and the Aldwych. It moved on to Westminster, not St John's parish, originally selected because of the threat to (Lord) North Street, but St Margaret's (Vols X, XIII and XIV). This parish covered not only most of the historic site of the magnificent Whitehall Palace and the Banqueting Hall [**29**], but also most major government offices, including Nos 10 and 11 Downing Street, photographed for the volume by permission of the then Prime Minister, Stanley Baldwin [**30**, **31**]. It, too, had its share of 'threatened buildings', and even buildings already demolished, like those in Storey's Gate cleared away for the Home Office building [**32**], were included. From St Margaret the Survey of London moved logically to St Martin-in-the-Fields (Vols XVI, XVIII and XX) to cover the rest of Whitehall, and then to the Strand, where, sadly, the loss of the Adelphi Estate provided the buildings-at-risk element.

The case of the Adelphi illustrates the co-operation between Council and Committee. Once parliamentary approval for demolition had been given, it was

Lovell who went to see A B Hayward, Surveyor to the Adelphi Estate, to consult him on the 'best surviving staircases, ceilings and fireplaces'. It was also Lovell who researched the historic drawings and arranged for the ceilings and other details to be recorded by A E Gurney under the Unemployed Architects' Scheme.[67]

On the other hand, on occasion, Council employees were active in carrying out documentary research to assist the London Survey Committee. This assistance was manifested as early as 1914, when Braines was thanked for research in the Record Office for Volume VI on Hammersmith, and it is clear that the final Committee volume, XXIV, on the (St Pancras) King's Cross Neighbourhood, would never have appeared without assistance from both the Council and the NBR. However high feelings ran on the Joint Publishing Committee, relations between Lovell and Godfrey and the Council staff always seem to have been cordial, and both Braines and Ida Darlington became members of the Active Committee.

The Survey Committee, to whom heraldry had always been of importance, had always set great store by the recording of monuments, and a large number were recorded. Even before colour reproduction was in any way practical, some of the early monograph volumes had hand-coloured heraldic plates. Expert help on the matter of heraldry was provided by the Revd Edward Earle Dorling (1864–1943), whose 'interest in heraldic matters and exceptional skill as a draughtsman' led him

30 *The Cabinet Room at No. 10 Downing Street, photographed in 1927 for the London County Council, by permission of the then Prime Minister, Mr Stanley Baldwin*

31 *The dining room at No. 11 Downing Street, photographed in 1927*

to abandon regular parochial work for that of heraldic adviser, first to the *Victoria County History*, and then to the newly founded Royal Commission for Historical Monuments for England. He was responsible for the accuracy and elegant presentation of the heraldic blazons for both Council and Committee volumes in the 1920s and 1930s.[68] The Council seems to have taken this preoccupation seriously, and paid fulsome tribute to Dorling's scholarship, old-fashioned though it may have seemed.

The Committee's approach had been set out by Godfrey in his first volume on Chelsea:

> *This is the proper place to remind those who are imperfectly acquainted with our Survey work that the chief object of these books is to illustrate by photographs and drawings all that is of special historic or aesthetic value in the districts surveyed. The subjects illustrated are briefly described in the letterpress, and as much historical information as could be placed within the slender compass of our space has been added in the form of notes . . . The text, however, must be understood to be subservient to the plates, which actually constitute our Survey of Chelsea.[69]*

In 1914 the Committee submitted a schedule relating to the content and format of volumes, approved by the Joint Publishing Committee on 22 June 1914 as 'Detailed Instructions as to the Content and Format of the Parish Surveys' (*see* Appendix 2). This set out some criteria familiar to the members of the Survey Committee: the civil parish (boundaries to be as in 1894); the area (to which, however, more than one volume could be devoted); the schedule (or register, to include 'every building and object of art or craftsmanship having a permanent position in the parish and dating from . . . before . . . 1800'). Later objects had to be approved by the Publishing Committee. Illustrations could include photographs, sketches, measured drawings and details, and were to include the relevant section of the Ordnance Survey map. The historical and descriptive notes, to be related to the schedule of buildings, were to include the names of the ground landlord, etc, condition of the building, description of fabric according to a certain formula and details of the tenants compiled from ratebooks, heads of institutions, etc. As far as buildings were concerned, a list of details to be checked and recorded was provided. Though it seems clear that this formula gradually proved impracticable, as well as unsympathetic to some authors, it did provide a pro forma which made it possible to make use of relatively untrained labour on a vast project.[70]

32 *Storey's Gate and Great George Street, Whitehall, before the demolition of the north side*

33 *Montagu House, designed by*
William Burn in 1859–62, and
demolished in 1951

The first Council volumes attempted to pursue the ideal of the annotated survey, but the frustration of scholars and historians wishing to paint a broader picture of the locality breaks through. In Volume VIII, *The Parish of St. Leonard, Shoreditch*, a historical introduction replaced the biographical and historical notes, partly because of the disjointed nature of the material but largely because of the difficulty of relating it to a specific site. It was felt that in the course of research 'a large amount of information had been collected which could not otherwise have been utilised'.[71] It was also the Council volumes which broke the '1800 barrier', and brought later buildings into the Survey. In the second St Margaret volume (XIII), of which a large part was dedicated to Whitehall Palace, also covered were the 19th-century buildings about to be demolished for the new War Ministry buildings – Nos 1–6 Whitehall Gardens, Richmond Terrace, and even the outrageously Victorian Montagu House (1859–62) by William Burn [**33**].

Even keeping up with, let alone competing with, this greater depth of research created strains for the Survey Committee, despite the informal help it received from Council employees. The correspondence between Lovell and Godfrey in the 1930s records the problems, probably made more acute by the heavy load they were both carrying.

34 *The interior of the church of All Hallows, Barking-by-the-Tower, in 1875, with its plaster ceiling of 1814*

35 *The interior of the church of All Hallows c 1910, as altered, with box pews cut down and contemporary timber roof*

36 *All Hallows, Barking-by-the-Tower, the organ case, measured and drawn by G Gordon Godfrey and Percy Lovell*

It is clear, also, that a coherent policy on the choice of parishes to be covered was more difficult for a voluntary group dependent on the goodwill and personal enthusiasm of its members. Thus, after Volume IV, *The Parish of Chelsea (Part II)*, had been published in 1913, and Volume VI, *The Parish of Hammersmith*, published in 1915, the choice of parishes seems to have become somewhat opportunist. The Hammersmith volume, started by Percy Lovell, who had then enlisted, had been completed in the early years of the First World War by Godfrey with the help of Braines over some of the research.

After the War, the Survey Committee had turned to the City. A W Clapham, an old friend of Godfrey, and later Secretary of the RCHME, with Minnie Reddan, who had covered the priory for the Victoria County History, had written a single volume (IX) on *The Church of St. Helen, Bishopsgate*. Volume XII, *The Church of All Hallows, Barking-by-the-Tower* (1929), had been covered [**34**, **35**, **36**], largely through the support of the Revd P T B Clayton, better known as 'Tubby' Clayton of

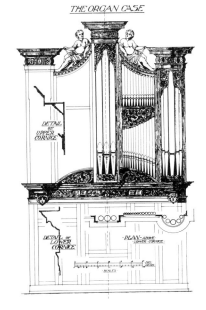

THE ORGAN CASE

37 *Moreton House, No. 14 South Grove, Highgate, section through staircase, measured and drawn by Cynthia Wood*

Toc H fame, for whom Lilian J Redstone had researched the text in 1925–6. The help of several 'outside' scholars was enlisted, and Marjorie Honeybourne (c 1900–74), later Editor and a leading figure in the LTS,[72] worked on Volume XV, *The Parish of All Hallows, Barking-by-the-Tower. (Part II)*, and Eliza Jeffries Davis (1875–1943) on the St Pancras volumes [**37**].

Lovell's experience in dealing with the latter, a most distinguished London historian and a founding member of the Institute of Historical Research,[73] epitomises the problems for the editor working with amateurs. Godfrey seems to have been the recipient of both parties' confidences: 'This is the fourth evening since I received the footnotes, on 19 July, that I have sat up till 1am or later, over those proofs!', complained EJD, on 28 July 1938, adding: 'The work as a whole is depressing: quite unlike what one anticipated, from the admirable scheme drafted by Mr Lovell at the end of 1936.' In a weary letter to Godfrey, on 3 November, Lovell put his side of the case:

> After a long morning with the JD and an afternoon getting clear about all she said, I handed in the book for better for worse, for richer for poorer to the Darlington.
>
> If we had another revise we should have exactly as many alterations and corrections as we made on this one. The lady said she did not wish to appear on the list of active members as she had 'grave doubts' as to everything Marcham writes, but will pay a guinea, so I put her among the subscribers. Yet at the same time she wants badly to write that third volume, and if only we could be sure that we could get the historical portion in time, I believe she knows more about the district than any of us and that she would do it well. Actually I believe also that what she really objects to is all this early medieval stuff that we put in now, and wants to get the Survey back to its true formation. A record of buildings up to roughly 100 years ago and a few historical notes about the sites, which was what we really did in Highgate or at any rate tried to . . .
>
> A third volume should be a definite survey again and mainly a town-planning one except for one or two obvious gaps. There is very little early history to deal with . . .
>
> PS Any how the Lady now receives no notices of the Active Committee and we can feel free to discuss the next volume without interference.[74]

The four volumes on Chelsea, being almost wholly written by Godfrey, caused no such problems. The first two (Vol II, *The Parish of Chelsea (Part I.)*, and Vol IV, *Chelsea. (Part II)*) dealt with the houses remaining from before 1800, and follow the Survey Committee style, with details of contemporary landlord, leaseholder and occupier, and the names of well-known ratepayers until the end of the 18th century. Volume VII dealt with the Old Church, which Godfrey's firm rebuilt after it was bombed in the Second World War, and Volume XI with the Royal Hospital. Though scholarly and competent within their limits, the volumes leave out much that is of interest in Chelsea today, and this is a parish which has often been cited as a case for revision.

Survey Committee draughtsmen

The drawings in the monographs and the Survey Committee parish volumes were by a number of draughtsmen. They include Lovell, Godfrey, his brother G Gordon Godfrey, a talented water-colour painter, and his partner Edmund Wratten, and assistants from their office, notably T Oliver Thirtle (1892–1981). Some draughtsmen worked on the Survey over a surprisingly long time, including Edwin Gunn ARIBA, Percy K Kipps, Francis R Taylor LRIBA, Philip S Hudson ARIBA and

NORTH·ELEVATION·
(FACING·HIGH·ST·)

38 *The Spotted Dog in Poplar High
Street, an old half-timbered inn,
recorded in 1894 by Ernest
Godman, Secretary of the London
Survey Committee*

Albert E Bullock, a specialist in ceilings. In other cases, one man seems to have worked almost exclusively on a single volume, like A E Gurney, who did most of the work on Volume XV, *The Parish of All Hallows, Barking-by-the-Tower. (Part II)*.

There had been a rapid accumulation of surveys and drawings in the early days, which enabled the Survey Committee to claim in its 1906 Report that it held 'a very large and beautiful collection of drawings, sketches, measured work, etc.', some 2,500 items in all, 'mounted and arranged in great albums according to the parishes of London' on the lines of the Crace collection. This meant that some early drawings were not used for many years – a measured drawing by Ernest Godman of 'the Spotted Dog, Poplar, 1894' [**38**] is to be used at last in Volume XLIII, *All Saints, Poplar*. Not all draughtsmen were members of the Active Committee. The list does not include the names of A F Lodge and A Down, whose drawings were used for the Swakeleys volume [*see* **27**, **28**]; others went on to distinction in other fields, such as the architects, L C T Moore (1883–1957), W Arthur Webb (1861–1923), who wrote the monograph *Sandford Manor, Fulham* (1907), and Frank Baines, later architect to ICI.

Though it is possible to discover who produced the text and drawings for the Committee volumes, it is more difficult to discover who drew for the Council volumes. The tradition of anonymity for officers in the public service was very strong, and in the earlier volumes measured drawings are austerely credited (like other drawings from the Architect's Department), to 'The Architect to the Council'. It was not until Topham Forrest's reign (1919–35) that any name emerges from the Architect's Department, and then these are probably those of managers rather than of draughtsmen. In *St. Leonard, Shoreditch* (1922) C J T Dadd is thanked for his help, in Volume XIV he is 'assisted' and then, in Volume XVI, replaced by W Dathy Quirke. Only after the Second World War do the names of individual draughtsmen emerge, such as Frank Evans [**39**], who did so much to establish a tradition of fine measured drawings for the Council volumes in the Sheppard era.[75]

GROUND FLOOR 72

FIRST FLOOR 72

FEET METRES 10 0 10 20 30 / 3 0 3 6 9

70

39' 0"

38' 6"

72 OXFORD GARDENS 50

55

CAMBRIDGE GARDENS

LADBROKE GROVE

FEET METRES 10 0 10 / 3 0 3

ARCHITRAVE
Ground Floor

6"

SKIRTING

EXTERNAL BRACKET

1' 3"

ARCHITRAVE

6"

STAIR BALUSTER

2' 8"

Ground Floor FIREPLACE Front Room
marble and tiles

3' 3⅝"

RAILINGS

2' 10"

39 *No. 72 Oxford Gardens, plans, elevations and details, measured and drawn by F A Evans*

43

The Unemployed Architects' Scheme

There had been one interesting initiative in the 1930s, when Lovell with typical ingenuity had made capital out of a difficult situation. During the First World War the London Society had employed architects who were not fit enough to go to the Front, and were unemployed, in preparing zoning maps for town-planning schemes.[76] In 1915 Ashbee had made an unsuccessful appeal to Gomme for the Council to pay for buildings to be measured by unemployed architects.[77] When in the 1920s it had been generally acknowledged that the Survey was falling behind, Ashbee had produced a stillborn scheme characterised as 'madcap' by Lovell, under which 'no London man should take his ARIBA without preparing a survey of a district of London on the lines of our survey volumes'. 'Who's going to teach all these students?', demanded Lovell in strong disapproval.[78]

With the advent of the slump in the 1930s, the Royal Institute of British Architects (RIBA) acted swiftly, on the pattern of the earlier scheme, to help its members threatened by 'serious and increasing unemployment'; the result was a project not dissimilar to the Historic American Buildings Survey [**40**]. The HABS, as it is known, was started as a Civil Works Administration scheme in November 1933, to provide for similarly unemployed US architects. Where, of course, it differs from the Unemployed Architects' Scheme is that it is still in existence, supported by organisations both public and private, at both federal and state level.

The British scheme was started by the RIBA and the London Society in the

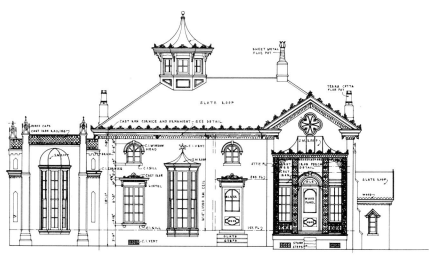

40 *David Dale Owen House, New Harmony, Indiana, USA, built 1859 by the son of Robert Owen, the British social reformer. Drawn for the Historic American Buildings Survey, 1934*

David Dale Owen House, south elevation

capital in response to a letter from Raymond Unwin to members of the Institute. The idea was to use redundant architects 'to carry further the survey and planning of London, with special reference to providing practical suggestions for the clearance of slums and for the improvement of the City, which may be a guide for the future'. They were to work on a zoning plan to guide redevelopment under the expected Town and Country Planning Act. It was to be funded by a levy on architects and their staff still in work.[79]

The plan was managed in the London area with characteristic vigour by Lovell, who, discovering that the larger schemes would take some time to get going, offered to set men to work on the recording of threatened buildings, to assist the Committee and the LCC in carrying out their surveys.[80] The scheme started on 18 January 1932, and by 1 February an ecstatic Lovell could write to Godfrey:

> *The scheme grows slowly from day to day and I now have 21 men helping, 18 of them measuring old buildings, 2 on zoning and 1 (who lives far out at Leigh-on-Sea) starting on the 'Register of Ancient Monuments', which has never been seriously tackled and got into manageable form with an index so you can turn up any house or monument at a moment and see what the position is . . .*

> *. . . I am also slowly absorbing the best men from the LCC's own temporary staff, 200 of whom have been dismissed. If we had only got enough funds we could measure up the whole of the old houses in London in a year! It is a most astonishing and unexpected development.[81]*

The source for the proposed 'Register of Ancient Monuments' was the information on historic buildings given in the RCHME volumes; so perhaps one can see in it the beginnings of the NBR so effectively created by Godfrey during the war years. The index can be seen as the forerunner of the computerised 'national heritage database' still being built up by the RCHME.[82]

The results of this are a surprising collection of drawings, all stamped 'Drawn for the London Society, copyright RIBA', eventually acquired by Godfrey for the NBR. They are a remarkable and catholic collection, not all of whose subjects have disappeared. Thus, though we have the staircase from Chesterfield House [**41**, **42**] and the modest house that closed the northern end of Savile Row [**43**], whose disappearance left room for Fortress House, we also find Sutton House, Hackney, Battersea House, in whose survival the London Society also had a hand [see **24**], St John's School, Wapping, and houses on the north side of Clapham Common. Possibly most extraordinary to find on the list of threatened buildings is a range of fine houses in Upper Mall, Chiswick, whose extinction was threatened by the Cromwell Road extension, originally conceived as running along the river.

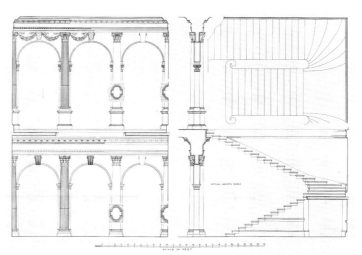

41 *Chesterfield House, Mayfair, designed by Isaac Ware in 1748–9 for the Fourth Earl of Chesterfield; the staircase c 1894*

42 *Chesterfield House, Mayfair; the staircase was recorded in the 1930s under the aegis of the London Society. It was demolished in 1937*

Nowhere is this co-operation between the London Society and the London Survey Committee more fruitful, as many of the originals used in both monograph and parish volumes appear under the name of the London Society in the NBR accession lists. Even some of the Council volumes made use of drawings provided by the London Society, such as the drawings of the Adelphi neighbourhood in Volume XVIII, *The Strand (St. Martin-in-the-Fields. Part II)* (1937) [**44**].

Survey of London drawings

It is not clear where all the drawings are today, either those created specifically for the Survey of London volumes or those recorded under the Unemployed Architects' Scheme. W H Godfrey seems to have acquired a large number for the NBR in the early years of the collection. This includes a great deal of London Society material, accessioned to the NBR in 1947,[83] but it is unlikely that this is exhaustive, because other material, which can be identified through reproductions, is catalogued under the names of individuals. The material from the London Survey Committee collection appears to have been deposited, or at any rate accessioned, in 1949,[84] including some of the artwork for the early volumes. Again it is not clear that all the material was intended for specific Survey of London volumes, but could have been drawn in anticipation for the original register, for which recording was carried out very widely. There were also engravings and original drawings listed which seem to have been later withdrawn, possibly because they were only deposited for safety in the war years, and they may have been the personal property of Ashbee.[85]

No 23 SAVILE ROW, W.1

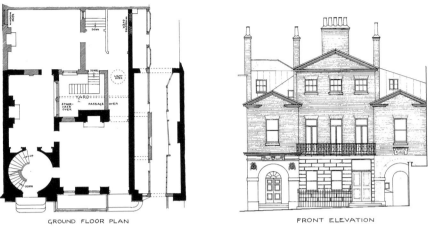

GROUND FLOOR PLAN

FRONT ELEVATION

SCALE OF FEET

43 *No. 23 Savile Row and the adjacent buildings were demolished in the 1930s to open up a cul-de-sac in the interests of traffic. The elevation and plan of No. 23 Savile Row were measured and drawn under the aegis of the London Society*

ELEVATION

44 *Elevation of Nos 17 and 18 Buckingham Street, a measured drawing prepared for the London Society*

The drawings made by Council draughtsmen, for the Council and Committee volumes during the period 1912–52, and for Council volumes thereafter, remained in the care of the Architect's Department until 1986. The majority of these seem to have been retained by the Historic Buildings Division, and thus transferred to English Heritage in due course, though yet others may have been stored in the Architect's Plan Room at County Hall.

Problems on the Joint Publishing Committee

One problem was the provision of 'free' copies of Council volumes to the members of the Survey Committee. This was much disliked by the LCC, which doubted the Committee's record-keeping, on one occasion complaining that books were given 'to people who have been dead for years', which Lovell found 'a delightful though irritating exaggeration'.[86]

There were more profound problems, however, over the differing approaches of the two sets of authors. From the signing of the 1910 agreement, the parish volumes assumed a deceptive uniformity which masked some fundamental differences between Council and Committee, and considerable changes over the period. It was the Survey Committee which had ensured the agreement of guidelines by the Joint Publishing Committee in 1914, but, as has been shown, the differing approaches of the two groups, and the greater use of documentary sources by the professional historians employed by the Council, made the two sets of volumes different in style and emphasis. The matter came to a head in 1935, after the agreement between the Council and the Committee had come up for renewal, and been extended for a year, partly because, in Lovell's words, 'Braines' book would otherwise have gone to the wall'.[87] The choice of a new parish caused Lovell some disquiet, and a certain amount of dissension on the Joint Publishing Committee, where the sympathetic Meinertzhagen had been replaced as Chairman by the cantankerous MacDonnell, castigated by Lovell as 'our old 2nd hand furniture dealer Macd'.[88] The Committee was embarking on the parish of St Pancras, Part I of which, *The Village of Highgate* (Vol XVII), was to appear in 1936. From Lovell's correspondence to Godfrey and the latter's to E P Wheeler, Architect to the Council from 1935 to 1939, and an old friend, it becomes clear that the Council felt that the Committee's volumes had too little popular appeal, and were too much confined to the buildings. Percy Lovell expressed his views to Godfrey on a characteristic postcard: 'I have no stomach for an Advisory Committee producing a biennial volume written by LCC officials on lines devised by MacDonnell . . . I think the whole point is that they want a *history* of London district by district, we must have a survey of monuments parish by parish.'[89]

In a private letter to Wheeler, Godfrey admitted that, though the Committee welcomed the 'recent detailed histories' produced by 'the Clerk's department, under Braines' guidance', it had not the means to do the research. The original purpose had been 'to publish a full architectural record of the historical buildings of London', and a 'full documentary record' of the parish was not anticipated. The Committee's chief concern was 'that the Survey should not be dropped or so altered in its character as to be virtually discontinued'. Acknowledging that 'your own department has always appreciated the Committee's aim, and . . . your draughtsmen and photographers are as fitted as ourselves . . . for carrying out the Survey', he said that the Committee would not be unhappy if the Council took the project over, provided it did not change character.[90]

A number of ideas for reorganising the approach to the Survey were discussed between Lovell and Godfrey, including abandoning to the LCC the contentious parish volumes in the County of London, with their unpalatable emphasis on history, getting the City to cover its own parishes, and allowing the Survey Committee to concentrate on the monographs.[91] These were altogether more attractive to amateur authors, much easier to manage, and required far less in the way of trained manpower. The resources in historians, archivists and medieval specialists which the study of urban history was beginning to demand were making it more and more difficult for the Survey Committee to produce volumes as substantial and well researched as those of the Council.

The crisis appears to have passed, possibly because more serious crises loomed, and Lovell immersed himself in the sometimes thankless task of preparing the St Pancras volumes. He did a good deal of research himself, reporting to Godfrey on the second St Pancras volume, *Old St. Pancras and Kentish Town* (Vol XIX), in the early part of 1938: 'I've done the rate-books for the 3 terraces and refuse to do any more. The residents are a dull lot of nonentities as far as one can judge except for a Portuguese chap who lived in 5 houses at the same time.'[92]

In July 1939, despite the Council's increasing preoccupation with the coming war, he was continuing with his work, offering to borrow a chauffeur and car and drive Godfrey round the area.[93] A month later he was complaining in words which strike an occasional chord with any architectural historian: 'I am sweating at the survey of streets and trying to draft my notes comprehensibly . . . Its weary work & you get so tired of all the railings & it is very hard to make a comprehendable [*sic*] let alone interesting description.'[94]

On 2 September 1939 Miss Crum, Lovell's secretary for nearly thirty years, dutifully sent out the postcards for the meeting on 16 September 1939. However, on that day Lovell was in Torquay, whither he had been evacuated from his house at Orford in Suffolk, and Godfrey had business elsewhere. The latter's telegram read: 'Very sorry prevented from coming today, Godfrey'.[95]

THE WINDING-UP OF THE SURVEY COMMITTEE, 1940–1952

The outbreak of war in 1939 signalled the suspension of the Survey Committee's activities, though quarterly meetings were held in the rooms provided for the London Society at the British Museum.[96] Godfrey, though he did not abandon the Survey of London, took up the post of Director of the National Buildings Record, a project which was to absorb much of his energy for the rest of his life. Percy Lovell went to Leicester for family reasons, throwing himself into the work of the Diocesan Advisory Committee, and the recording of local buildings for the NBR. Increasing ill health kept him from returning to London, but his memorial is in the London Society library, to which he left all his London books, including a splendid set of Survey of London volumes bound in white vellum. The rooms in Lancaster House had to be abandoned for a series of lodgings in various government buildings.

Though the war was far from over, in 1944 an attempt was made to mark the fiftieth anniversary of the founding of the Survey. A report was issued in which the achievements and aims of the Committee were summarised: despite difficulties the Survey Committee had produced fifteen monographs, and, together with the LCC, twenty parish volumes, though with more support much more of London could have been properly documented. It was emphasised that its volumes would be helpful in post-war reconstruction – for instance, two churches 'of the first importance' had been destroyed by enemy action, but peace-time records of their structure were available. But there was no room for complacency:

Damage by war is however by no means the worst danger, nor the most persistent, that threatens our architectural inheritance. Development and improvement schemes, business enterprise, the fortunes and hazards in the lives of owners and tenants, are all fraught with risk to buildings and the need of adequate records is more urgent today than ever.[97]

With extraordinary panache and energy Godfrey also produced, with the financial help of the Pilgrim Trust, a monograph volume, *The Church of St. Bride, Fleet St* [**45**]. Quite apart from his own heavy burden at the NBR, the preparation and writing presented considerable problems. The church had been bombed, so physical recording was difficult, and he had to depend on existing surveys; even the records were unavailable in safe storage, and he had to rely on another's notes.

Godfrey remained Director of the NBR until 1960, and was also a member of a number of other official bodies, including, most appropriately, the Advisory Committee on Buildings of Special Architectural and Historic Interest which

45 *St Bride, Fleet Street, in 1944, after bombing in the Blitz*

advised the Minister of Housing on listing. He found time to round off the work of the Survey Committee by bringing to a conclusion the work done on St Pancras. The third volume on the parish, Volume XXI, *Tottenham Court Road and Neighbourhood* (1949), was to a large extent the work of others. It was started by W McB Marcham, assisted by John Summerson, then a colleague at the NBR, who

46 *Euston Station: the famous entrance, later mourned as the demolished 'Euston Arch'*

wrote up Euston Station [**46**] and University College, while J W Bloe FSA (d 1965), a member of the RCHME's staff who was on the Active Committee, did the Percy Street area.[98] The drawings sometimes came from existing collections, or were occasionally by amateurs, but were largely carried out by Miss B G Bryan Brown of the NBR. The Council also played its part: Ida Darlington, who had become a full member of the Active Committee, and her department assisted with research, while the Council collections provided most of the photographs and even the occasional drawing. A sign of the times was the appointment by the LCC of an assistant expressly to carry out research on Committee volumes.[99]

Volume XXIV, the last part of St Pancras, *King's Cross Neighbourhood*, had been begun by Lovell and was again completed by Godfrey and Marcham. J W Bloe again did much of the listing of the surviving houses and the notes on their condition, while Summerson did the same for the churches. The accounts of the building estates were provided by Hugh Phillips FSA (1886–1972), an authority and writer on mid Georgian London, who also published very successful historical novels on the same period under the sobriquet of 'Philip Hughes'.[100] The Council provided both research and measured surveys for standing buildings [**47**].

In 1952 the London Survey Committee made it clear that its members were no longer able to continue the work on the Joint Publishing Committee, and the Council decided to end the arrangement. At the same time, the decision was

47 *Nos 42–58 and 33–49 Frederick Street were built by Thomas and William Cubitt in 1823–7. These elevations were measured and drawn by A J North*

taken to transfer the responsibility for the Survey within the Council. In 1934 the Local Government, Records and Museums Committee had been wound up, and the historical buildings transferred to the Parks Committee, the Survey remaining with the Library under the Establishment Committee. Now it was proposed that the Survey of London should join 'historical buildings and antiquarian objects' as part of the remit of the newly created Architectural and Historical Subcommittee of the Town Planning Committee. The Subcommittee would be able to co-opt advisers from outside the Council, entitled to speak but not to vote.[101]

In a valedictory piece about the Survey Committee, in the *London Topographical Record*, Godfrey gave the reasons for its winding-up:

> *Recruits for the heavy unpaid work which an earlier generation undertook with enthusiasm are no longer forthcoming, but our efforts will not have been in vain, if . . . the great governing body of the County of London continues the work . . . Now that a paid editor has been appointed the work should go forward with less strain.*[102]

The drawings had already in large part been deposited in the NBR; the remaining funds of the Survey Committee were given to the LTS, of which Godfrey had been Chairman and Editor since 1928,[103] while some years later the minutes and other office records were deposited with the Greater London Record Office.

THE COUNCIL YEARS, 1952–1986

If, through the tenor of the times, the Survey Committee was unable to continue, the project lost Ida Darlington through the expansion of her department. She had succeeded to Braines's place on the Survey in 1935, and was also responsible for the management of the Members' Library, much enriched by the gift of John Burns' Library in 1943[104] and gradually transformed by her own efforts into a specialist collection of London books. She was responsible for the last Westminster volume, XX, *Trafalgar Square and Neighbourhood* (St Martin-in-the-Fields. Part III), published in 1940. Her department was already supporting the Committee volumes, and produced the two South Bank volumes – XXII, *Bankside (The Parishes of St. Saviour and Christ Church, Southwark*, and XXIII, *South Bank and Vauxhall (The Parish of St. Mary, Lambeth, Part I)* – in 1950 and 1951. After the decision by the Survey Committee to cease producing volumes on the appearance of Volume XXIV, Volume XXV, *St. George's Fields (The Parishes of St. George the Martyr and St. Mary Newington, South-wark)*, appeared in 1955, under her own name, uniquely among LCC parish volumes.

48 *Francis Sheppard, General Editor of the Survey of London 1954–83*

In view of Ida Darlington's increasing workload as Head of the LCC Record Office and Library, to her great regret, after twenty years' association with the Survey of London,[105] the decision to appoint a new full-time Council editor was taken. From a strong field of 154 applicants, Francis Sheppard [**48**], an Assistant Keeper at the Museum of London, was selected to take up the new post of General Editor.

The Historic Buildings Panel

Sheppard was fortunate in leading the Survey of London during a period when the Council attached great importance to the whole question of conservation and the maintenance of historic buildings, and indeed earned international renown for its performance in these fields. This had begun in the great post-war period of town planning and historic buildings conservation under an early Chairman, Robert Fiske, and the LCC and its successor, the Greater London Council (GLC), time and again demonstrated its interest in preserving historic buildings. Despite the competing claims of public housing, private developers and the need for improved roads, the Historic Buildings Panel (as it is best known) showed its ability to put a bipartisan approach to good use from Roehampton to Covent Garden. In the words of the London MP Patrick Ground, 'the historic buildings committee has been very good for London, by ensuring that thousands of historic buildings, which otherwise might have been threatened have survived. It has also done a great deal in retaining London's character and quality.'[106] Under chairmen as diverse as Mrs Chaplin and Lady Dartmouth, Louis Bondy and William Bell, it controlled development, administered historic houses, distributed grants, recorded threatened buildings and put up blue plaques, in order to save and celebrate London's historic buildings.

As Edward Leigh, a Conservative MP and former GLC member pointed out, it also provided 'an example of distinguished men and women being brought into local government service'.[107] The Panel had an eminent group of co-opted advisers throughout the period, including T F Reddaway, Lord Faringdon (1902–77), Lord Reilly, and, most notably, that doughty quartet of architectural knights, Sir Osbert Lancaster [**49**], Sir John Betjeman [**50**], Sir John Summerson [**51**] and Sir Hugh Casson.

The publishing of the Survey of London was an integral part of this campaign: though the original register had been superseded by the Government Lists of Buildings of Architectural and Historic Interest, the Survey's research enhanced the descriptions and amplified knowledge about known historic buildings. Its drawings and architectural descriptions enabled restoration to be carried out in a manner more scholarly and authentic, while the collaboration between researchers and architects in the Council employ informed the work of both.

The Survey of London was usually housed with its fellow department, the Historic Buildings Division of the Architect's Department, under two successive Surveyors of Historic Buildings, W A Eden (1963–70) and B Ashley Barker

49 *Sir Osbert Lancaster*

50 *Sir John Betjeman*

51 *Sir John Summerson*

(1970–86). After 1965 this was often in some remote outstation of the GLC rather than in County Hall itself. The Division managed the threatened buildings recording for the London area, and its architects controlled demolition and alterations to historic buildings. With access to district surveyors at one end of the spectrum, and architectural historians at the other, an impressive *corpus* of knowledge about London building practices developed.

Francis Sheppard, General Editor 1954–1983

Sheppard took up his post on 1 January 1954, and during his twenty-nine-year tenure some sixteen volumes were published, covering some of the richest and most varied parts of the metropolis. A number of technical and organisational changes were made. The Athlone Press, then the official publishing house of the University of London, took on the production of the volumes, which assumed a new double-column layout for the text, with figures integrated in the text. Plates returned to the familiar position at the back of the volumes (in Volume XXV signatures of photographs had been interspersed in the text).

The first area tackled was the second part of St Mary, Lambeth (Vol XXVI), and the preface was used to signal important changes of emphasis. First of all, there was a clear understanding that 'the Survey must take note of 19th-century buildings, to which many students of architecture have paid increasing attention in recent years'. Secondly, the residual war damage, and the threats from rebuilding throughout the County of London, indicated that there would have to be 'recording of threatened buildings in those parts . . . which have not yet been covered' to provide material for incorporation in future volumes.[108] The development of southern Lambeth took place largely in the 19th century, and members of the Survey team found themselves working on the study of suburban expansion, a pioneering enterprise to which H J Dyos paid tribute when he published his *Victorian Suburb* some five years later. In the words of John Summerson:

> The 'suburban sprawl' is no longer a figure of speech; it becomes something actual. This is important. The actuality of things forgotten (especially, perhaps, things despised) in the recent past, the truth under the surface of late assumptions, the seeing for the first time as historic *what has only lately been forgotten as* contemporary, *lies very near the root of creative thought and the formation of new attitudes.*[109]

Despite the success of the volume on suburban Lambeth, the Council decided that research should concentrate on central areas. The first was on the parishes of Christ Church and All Saints, Volume XXVII, which included Spitalfields, then about to be rediscovered [**52**]. After that the Council returned to Westminster, the central parishes of St James, St Anne, Soho, and St Paul, Covent Garden, all threatened in different ways by change. The four volumes on St James, Piccadilly, published in the 1960s, established the Survey's reputation as a work of urban history, building up a picture of the relations between the ground landlords, the developers and the individual builders. The detailed study of this rich part of the West End rolled back layer after layer of building to show the 16th-century landholdings and the 17th-century developments beneath the 19th-century clubs [**53**] and palaces.

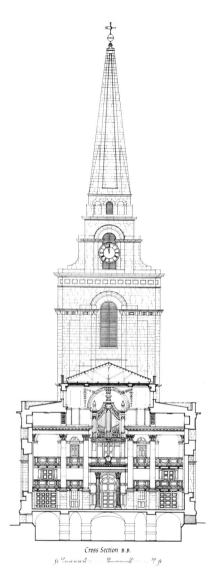

52 *Christ Church, Spitalfields, cross-section looking west, measured by F A Evans and Z Dmochowski and drawn by Mrs L F M Ison*

53 *The Reform Club, Pall Mall, designed by Sir Charles Barry; view of the saloon*

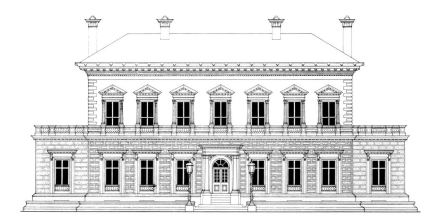

54 *No. 15 Kensington Palace Gardens, as in 1937–8, drawn by J J Sambrook*

55 *Royal Albert Hall, section looking towards the stage, redrawn by F A Evans*

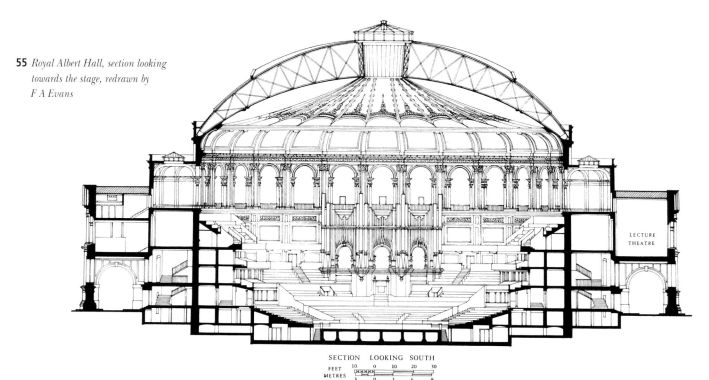

LECTURE
THEATRE

SECTION LOOKING SOUTH
FEET   10   0   10   20   30
METRES   3   0   3   6   9

In the early 1970s the Survey team broke new ground in its move to Kensington, essentially a series of Victorian suburban neighbourhoods built up on the outlying market gardens, brickfields and open spaces of a west London parish, very short on monuments in the original London Survey Committee sense, but bearing out the Council's decision to include Victorian buildings. In 1973, with the publication of Volume XXXVII on Northern Kensington, the Survey team demonstrated that an area developed in the Victorian period could be as fascinating as any medieval quarter [**54**]. The subsequent volume on *The Museums Area of South Kensington and Westminster* (XXXVIII) provided a masterly analysis, researched and written by Peter Bezodis, Deputy Editor of the Survey of London, of the workings of the Royal Commission for the 1851 Exhibition, the ground landlord for the area. It also provided a very detailed account of the construction of the various public buildings in the area. The South Kensington Museum was particularly concerned with innovative building methods, and this provided records of such major 19th-century monuments as the Royal Albert Hall [**55**] and the Natural History Museum.

Subsequently, the Survey of London was asked by the richest of the great London estates, that of the Duke of Westminster, to assist in the celebration of its tercentenary by using its archives to interpret and record the Mayfair estate [**56**]. This was a very interesting accolade, from a class of landowner which had not

56 *No. 66 Brook Street, Mayfair; internal elevation of a first-floor front room*

FRONT ELEVATION TO BALDERTON STREET

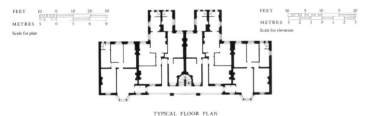

TYPICAL FLOOR PLAN

57 *Clarendon Flats, Balderton Street,*
erected by the Improved Industrial
Dwellings Company, to the designs
of 'Mr Robson'

58 *The conservatory in No. 75 South*
Audley Street in 1902, when
occupied by H L Bischoffsheim

always welcomed historians and researchers into its muniment room. It was also an indication that the Survey of London had truly arrived, and that its contribution to the understanding of the workings of the Grosvenor Estate was understood and appreciated. It provided a marvellous opportunity to study late 19th-century and even 20th-century building, since the Estate had always prided itself on keeping its properties up to date and properly maintained. Despite the grandeur of many of the establishments recorded, the Survey of London did not ignore the modest inhabitants, and model tenements [**57**] were recorded along with ballrooms and conservatories [**58**].

The interest in the inhabitants also becomes increasingly detailed. In the early volumes the Survey of London had perhaps given an undue emphasis to the armigerous; it had then turned to middle-class house-owners, and had then become much more democratic. Using the census returns, and later such sources as Charles Booth's *Life and Labour of the Poor*, it dealt with groups such as servants in middle-class homes, and at some length with working-class populations like the laundresses of Northern Kensington, and even the inmates of St Mary Abbots' Workhouse [**59**].

59 *St Mary Abbots' Workhouse, c 1880*

Sheppard's talents as Editor are amply shown by the scholarliness of the volumes, the quality of the staff he attracted, and the standing of the Survey as shown by reviews from historians and conservationists. The mutual respect and liking of Sheppard and his staff were demonstrated by the special Festschrift edition of the *London Journal* published after his retirement.[110] The benefits to historians lay not only in the volumes themselves but in the way they opened up new methods and new fields of research material to other urban historians. In the newly fashionable field of urban history, the Survey of London again led the way, with Sheppard participating in the first Urban History Conference organised by H J Dyos at Leicester in 1966.[111]

Management in a large organisation is never simple, and, though the tensions of the Joint Publishing Committee had been eliminated, the traditional divide between the Clerk's and Architect's Departments persisted in that the writers and researchers were in the former, while the Architectural Editor, who provided the descriptions of the buildings, and the draughtsmen were responsible to the Architect. Occasionally, this differing line of command could be put to good use by a colleague, but in the event Sheppard's reign saw an increasingly close integration of the text, drawings and other illustrations. With the gradual emergence of a tradition of urban and architectural history, the distinction between general historical background and architectural description disappeared as far as the text of the volumes was concerned. The Survey of London has always been fortunate in its architectural contributors; after 1954 these included Walter Ison, James Stevens Curl and Andrew Saint, all writers of distinction in their own right.

The Survey of London volumes are illustrated with a large number of figures. These range from measured surveys of buildings, made on the spot, and drawn up afterwards, to carefully researched reconstructions, where information from several sources can be combined. Often the only information available on a vanished building is an architect's plan or a topographical print; occasionally sketches are more effective than scale drawings. In the early Survey of London volumes it is clear that the drawings were often produced by authors like Lovell or Godfrey, but by the 1950s a more specialised type of draughtsman had emerged, who tended to specialise in measurement and architectural illustration.

THE ABOLITION OF THE GLC AND THE MOVE TO THE RCHME

Francis Sheppard retired at the end of 1982, and was succeeded in October 1983 by Hermione Hobhouse, recruited from outside the Council staff. She remains General Editor in the centenary year.

With the campaign to abolish the GLC, all London institutions were plunged into uncertainty, but from the publication of the initial White Paper there was no doubt that the Survey of London would continue, largely due to the reputation which it had built up under Dr Sheppard's management and the generous support of devoted users from many different fields. It was, however, still a difficult and unsettling time for staff, most of whom had given many years of service to the Council and to London local government.

The decision that the RCHME should take over responsibility for the Survey of London was based on the similarity in roles and working practices of the two organisations. As Kenneth Baker reported to the parliamentary committee looking into the matter:

> the case for transfer to the RCHM centred on the long and historical relationship between the two organisations in the provision of an historical analytical survey . . . the RCHM . . . has a duty to record listed buildings under threat, which, effectively, is what is being done by the Survey.[112]

The last official occasion for the Survey of London under the 'great governing body of London' that had supported it for so long was the launch, in March 1986, in the presence of Tony Banks, last Chairman of the Greater London Council, of Volume XLII, *South Kensington: Kensington Square to Earl's Court*.

In April 1986 the Survey of London became part of the Royal Commission on the Historical Monuments of England. Since its move to the RCHME eight years ago, the Survey has settled into a new organisation, its staff has grown and so has the breadth of its coverage. Before Abolition, it was already at work on two new projects: the study of the East End parish of All Saints, Poplar, and a survey of County Hall.

County Hall was to be the first monograph undertaken by the Survey's own professional team – the earlier ones had been produced by the London Survey Committee. County Hall was clearly a 'threatened building' in that, having been designed as the headquarters of a local government body that had just been abolished, it was faced with the prospect of conversion to a wholly different purpose and hence very substantial change. The flagship rooms – the Council Chamber [**60**], the main committee rooms, the Members' Library, the Chairman's and Senior Officers' rooms – however sympathetically altered, would no longer

60 *The Council Chamber of County Hall as intended in 1911, from a water-colour by A C Horsnell, after the design by Ralph Knott*

61 *County Hall, competition entry*
by Edwin Lutyens

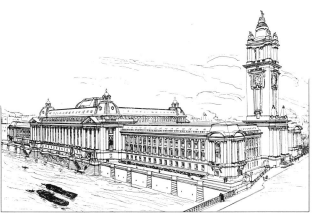

62 *County Hall, competition entry*
by Hinds & Deperthes

play their intended part in the management of London. Though much of the fine Edwardian and 1920s work had been torn out or covered up in the modernisation programme of the 1960s, a number of fine period details remained.

The design of the building had been decided by a competition held in 1907, entered by a number of well-known architects but won by an unknown, Ralph Knott. Because the building had been in a single ownership, the records both of design and of official management of the contract were all still available, giving a rare opportunity to look at the management of architectural competitions [**61**, **62**] and the relationship between architect and corporate patron. The building was carefully recorded by the Council's photographers before the abolition of the GLC, and information was supplemented by material from the Council's library of photographs. The monograph was published in 1991 and was in a sense a tribute to the LCC, which had been involved with the Survey of London for so long.

The completion of the parish of Kensington, the first complete parish to be surveyed in the thorough Sheppard fashion, left a wide field for the choice of the next parish. The final choice fell on the parish of All Saints, Poplar, but the decision was a difficult one.

An analysis of the areas that had already been covered by the Survey revealed both that there was still a large area of London to be researched and that, as this brief account has made clear, the coverage by the volumes varied very considerably in depth and analysis. It was also manifest, however, that the skills and techniques built up by the team had already assisted Londoners in understanding their own city, its construction and its history of development. The way in which these skills had been employed on the central areas of Westminster and the Victorian suburbs of Lambeth and Kensington had encouraged architectural historians and architects researching buildings to use those techniques on similar areas. It seemed clear that

63 *The West India Docks as proposed in 1802; aquatint by William Daniell*

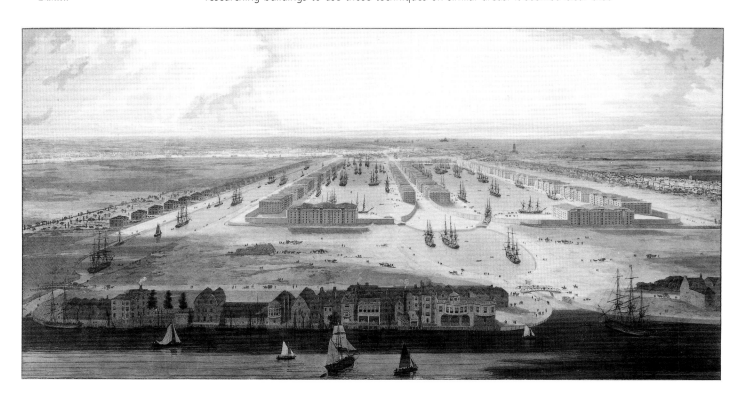

here was a 'pioneering' role for the Survey of London team: that is, by going into a parish or part of a parish, employing the skills and resources at its disposal to research it in depth, to locate the key sources and to establish a pattern of development, not only could it depict the development of that particular area; it could also illumine the ways in which similar areas could be investigated.

The 'fire-fighting' tradition of choosing areas according to the degree of threat to both the fabric and the changing way of life is a strong one in the Survey (as was shown by the first Council volume), and for this reason a docklands parish seemed the obvious choice. It fell on All Saints, Poplar, for several reasons: it was a clearly defined area, largely bounded by the Thames, on the east by the LCC boundary, and on the north by Bromley-by-Bow, the subject of Volume I. It also contained a very important early docks complex in the West India Docks [**63**], which together with the East India and Millbank Docks would give a comprehensive sample of dockland development in London. The presence of the London Docklands Development Corporation, and the inclusion of a large part of the area within the Enterprise Zone, made it clear that massive and irreversible change was to be expected, and that emergency recording would in any case be required.

It was clear, from the outset, that the project presented a considerable challenge, but with rapid change revolutionising an important industrial and port area which had been developed in the 19th century, it was a challenge that had to be faced [**64**, **65**]. It seemed important that such an area should be covered before

64 *Grieg House, Poplar, was built as a Sailors' Home to the design of Niven & Wigglesworth; elevation drawn by Mike Clements in 1986*

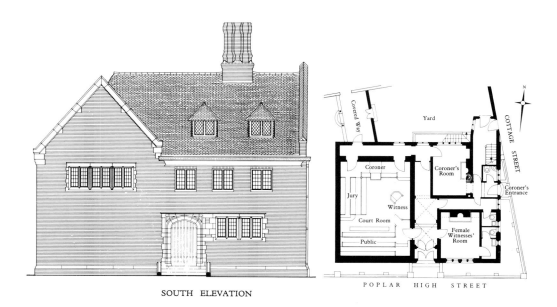

SOUTH ELEVATION

POPLAR HIGH STREET

65 *Poplar Coroner's Court, Poplar High Street, 1911, a modest civic building designed and built by the London County Council; elevation and plan redrawn by Ron New*

it was too late, and unlikely that any group of researchers without the accumulated expertise of the Survey team, let alone the funding of a government body, would have the capacity to tackle a comprehensive study of the parish. It could indeed be argued that it would have been a betrayal of the traditions of the Survey of London to have taken a more cautious route. Though it has taken longer than intended, it has provided a study of an important docklands area before it was hit by development on a scale unprecedented in east London. Comprehensive study was only possible *before* the buildings on the ground were largely obliterated by new development, but *after* the massive Port of London and dock companies' records had passed into the public domain. In the best traditions of Survey research, the team found itself new and unfamiliar sources – including, for instance, the Goad insurance maps, the Inland Revenue records for the 1910 Finance Act survey and even the field-books of Borough Valuers.

When the original Survey Committee had recorded parts of Poplar in 1894 [*see* **38**], it had seen it as a residual part of an old-established East End village. A century later the modern volume will deal not only with the 1951 Lansbury Festival of Britain development [**66**], now partly listed, but also with such recent developments as Cascades, a modern apartment block by Campbell, Zogolovitch,

Wilkinson & Gough, and the as yet incomplete Canary Wharf scheme, by the American architectural firm of Skidmore, Owings & Merrill. The team working on the area has also had to tackle the earlier story of the transformation of the marshy Isle of Dogs – from a feeding ground for animals taken to sea by the Navy in the 18th century, into a major docks complex with related industrial development, through decline to new development as middle-class housing and offices, a future which is not yet secure.

With Volumes XLIII and XLIV – *Poplar, Blackwall and the Isle of Dogs, the Parish of All Saints, Poplar* – in production, work has started on new areas. Considerable thought was given to their choice. Enough has been said of earlier discussions on similar occasions to make it unnecessary to rehearse the differing viewpoints in detail. The question of the size and type of area to be covered, the depth of coverage, the choice of area according to the age of the fabric and the period of the development, the quality or lack of it of the buildings, the degree of threat – all these were rehearsed. A new element was the acknowledgement that some of the earlier coverage, notably of the fashionable and much rebuilt Chelsea, was out of date, and that two centuries of building from 1800 to 1990 were likely to vanish without being recorded; resurvey of some parishes was therefore overdue.

Two themes stood out. The first was the need to record important central areas such as Bond Street, and such major landed estates as Portman and Harley-Cavendish in St Marylebone, before it was too late. The second was the necessity of looking at even newer suburbs – Tooting and other parts of south London, or Pinner and Kingsbury, part of Sir John Betjeman's beloved Metroland.

Three proposals were eventually presented to Commissioners and in due course approved: St John, Clerkenwell, a central parish with a medieval estate pattern, strong connections with the City and a history of modern development threatening its traditional small industries; the 'Knightsbridge Triangle', a small residential area of surprising richness; and Hyde Park and Kensington Gardens, the first 'open space' to be tackled by the Survey of London, where Survey staff are working in partnership with the Royal Commission's experienced field archaeologists in tracing the development of the landscape features. A study of the best method of tackling a 20th-century suburb is to be undertaken, in the interests of broadening the Survey's methods and coverage.

The Survey of London continues to serve London in recording the city's fabric as Ashbee and his friends intended a century ago, though in a slightly different fashion. Its development has moved from a band of enthusiasts, catechising postman, parson and schoolteacher, through full-blown historical research parish by parish as part of the civic government of the capital, to integration in the national body of survey and record, responsible for cataloguing the national archaeological and architectural fabric.

HOUSING

architect:

G. A. JELLICOE

F.R.I.B.A., M.T.P.I.

Perspective view from north of four storey blocks 14 and 15. Accommodation includes ground and first floor maisonettes : second and third floor maisonettes and flats. Plans are shown on pages 12 & 13

Three storey houses viewed from Grundy Street. Blocks 22, 23 and 24. The courtyard will be paved with no access for vehicular traffic. There will be flower gardens and seats. Accommodation includes 3-storey house ; ground floor bed-sitting room flats with upper floor maisonettes over. Plans are shown on page 14.

A patio roof garden to 3 room flats on the 3rd floor of Block 16. Below these flats are maisonettes.

66 *Lansbury Estate as designed, after a sketch by Geoffrey Jellicoe, from* The Architect and Building News, *9 June 1950*

Possibly, however, the greatest monument to the Survey of London lies in its example: in 1894 the Committee for the Survey of the Memorials of Greater London (to give it its original title) was advocating the making of a list of historic buildings with the intention of reducing ignorant and accidental destruction, a project taken up by local government. Twelve years later F J Horniman (1835–1906), a Liberal Cornish MP and Progressive LCC member for Chelsea, persuaded Campbell-Bannerman to set up 'a Commission . . . forthwith . . . to make an inventory of the Ancient and Historical Monuments . . . and to specify those . . . most worthy of preservation'. This initiative was always claimed by W H Godfrey to be in imitation of the Survey of London.[113] There were, of course, early personal links with the RCHME, through, for instance, A W Clapham (1883–1950), author and a member of the Active Committee, technical editor of the RCHME 1913–33, and Secretary 1933–48. The decision to pass responsibility for the Survey to the RCHME in 1986 was due to this 'long and historical relationship between the two organisations in the provision of a historical analytical survey'.[114]

With the Survey of London now an integral part of the Royal Commission, it is possible to look at its role today. The post-war Town and Country Planning Acts, and subsequent amendments, have provided the 'register' for which the Survey pioneers were working, while the Survey of London team and its colleagues elsewhere are working to provide the record of buildings, standing and 'threatened', which assists in the understanding of the country's heritage of buildings, and with other sources contributes to the stock of knowledge on which those registers are based.

It cannot be argued, however, that the work of the Survey of London is completed just because a national 'register' now exists. The official lists are available for the work of government at all levels, but they are of necessity dry and abbreviated. The Survey volumes provide a different sort of record for London, often used to amplify the official descriptions; very often the research that has created the Survey accounts has enabled official lists to be corrected. The volumes provide a work of reference for a wide band of users, from working architects to house-owners, from developers and builders to residents intrigued to know more about their homes. The Survey of London has moved from the recording of monuments to the interpretation of the urban fabric and this has meant moving forward both architecturally and in time to cover areas which have grown up since Ashbee's heroic and ambitious initiative.

Appendix 1 Volumes published for the Survey of London

The following list includes all the monographs and register (or parish) volumes published for the Survey of London. The diversity of authors and editors involved in these volumes over the last hundred years means that the approach is by no means consistent, but this reflects the varied influences on the Survey's development.

The matter cited below is taken from the main title page, unless otherwise indicated. LCC indicates a volume prepared by staff from the London County Council, LSC one prepared by members of the London Survey Committee.

PARISH VOLUMES

Volume	Publication date	Title details	
I	1900	The Survey of London; being the first volume of the Register . . . containing the Parish of Bromley-by-Bow.	
		Edited by C.R. Ashbee . . . and printed under the auspices of the London County Council	LSC
II	1909	The Parish of Chelsea (Part I.) by Walter H. Godfrey, Architect, being the second volume of the Survey of London	
		[No publisher or printer given]	LSC
III	1912	The Parish of St. Giles-in-the-Fields (Part I) being the third volume of the Survey of London, with Drawings, Illustrations and Architectural Descriptions, by W. Edward Riley, Architect to the Council.	
		Edited, with Introduction and Historical Notes, by Sir Laurence Gomme, Clerk of the Council	LCC
IV	1913	Chelsea. (Part II) . . . by Walter H. Godfrey, Member of the Committee for the Survey of the Memorials of Greater London	LSC
V	1914	St. Giles-in-the-Fields (Part II), being the fifth volume of the Survey of London . . . [as III]	LCC
VI	1915	The Parish of Hammersmith, being the sixth volume of the Survey of London. By the Members of the London Survey Committee.	LSC
VII	1921	The Old Church, Chelsea, being the seventh volume of the Survey of London. By Walter H. Godfrey, FSA, Member of The London Survey Committee	LSC
VIII	1922	The Parish of St. Leonard, Shoreditch, being the eighth volume . . . by G. Topham Forrest, Architect to the Council.	
		Edited . . . by Sir James Bird, Clerk to the Council.	LCC

IX	1924	The Church of St. Helen, Bishopsgate. being the ninth volume . . . by Minnie Redan and Alfred W. Clapham, FSA, Members of the London Survey Committee	LSC
X	1926	The Parish of St. Margaret, Westminster. Part I, being the tenth volume . . . by G. Topham Forrest.	
		Edited with historical notes by Montagu H. Cox, Clerk . . .	LCC
XI	1927	The Royal Hospital, Chelsea, being the eleventh volume . . . by Walter H. Godfrey, FSA, Member of the London Survey Committee	LSC
XII	1929	The Church of All Hallows, Barking-by-the-Tower. being the twelfth volume . . . by Lilian J. Redstone and Members of the London Survey Committee	LSC
XIII	1930	The Parish of St. Margaret, Westminster. Part II (Neighbourhood of Whitehall, vol. I). being the thirteenth volume of the Survey of London, by Montagu H. Cox, LLB. (LOND.) Clerk of the Council, and G. Topham Forrest, FRIBA, FRSE, FGS, Architect to the Council	LCC
XIV	1931	The Parish of St. Margaret, Westminster. Part III (Neighbourhood of Whitehall, vol. II), being the fourteenth volume . . . by Montagu H. Cox. and G. Topham Forrest . . .	LCC
XV	1934	The Parish of All Hallows, Barking-by-the-Tower. (Part II), being the fifteenth volume . . . by Members of the London Survey Committee.	LSC
XVI	1935	Charing Cross (The Parish of St. Martin-in-the-Fields. Part I), being the sixteenth volume of the Survey of London, by G.H. Gater, CMG, DSO, Clerk of the Council, and E.P. Wheeler, FRIBA, Architect to the Council	LCC
XVII	1936	The Village of Highgate (The Parish of St. Pancras. Part I), being the seventeenth volume . . . by Percy W. Lovell, FSA, and William McB. Marcham	LSC
XVIII	1937	The Strand (St. Martin-in-the-Fields. Part II), being the eighteenth volume . . . by Sir George Gater, CMG, DSO, Clerk, and E.P. Wheeler, FRIBA, Architect	LCC
XIX	1938	Old St. Pancras and Kentish Town (The Parish of St. Pancras. Part II), being the nineteenth volume . . . by Percy W. Lovell, FSA and W. McB. Marcham.	LSC
XX	1940	Trafalgar Square and Neighbourhood (The Parish of St. Martin-in-the-Fields. Part III) being the twentieth volume . . . by Sir George Gater, CMG, DSO, and F.H. Hiorns, FSA, FRIBA	LCC
XXI	1949	Tottenham Court Road and Neighbourhood (The Parish of St. Pancras. Part III), being the twenty-first volume . . . by Walter H. Godfrey, FSA, FRIBA, and W. McB Marcham	LSC
XXII	1950	Bankside (The Parishes of St. Saviour and Christ Church, Southwark), being the twenty-second volume of the Survey of London	LCC
XXIII	1951	South Bank and Vauxhall (The Parish of St. Mary, Lambeth, Part I), being the twenty-third volume of the Survey of London	LCC
XXIV	1952	King's Cross Neighbourhood (St. Pancras, Part IV), being the twenty-fourth volume of the Survey of London by Walter H. Godfrey, FSA, FRIBA, and W. McB Marcham	LSC

| XXV | 1955 | St. George's Fields (The Parishes of St. George the Martyr and St. Mary Newington, Southwark) being the twenty-fifth volume of the Survey of London   LCC |

[Sir Howard Roberts appears on the title page as General Editor and Ida Darlington is credited on the title page as author]

Henceforth F H Sheppard is credited as General Editor on the title page. No information on the authorship of the volumes is given formally, but the names of those involved from the Survey of London team are given in the individual prefaces. All the volumes are published by The Athlone Press for the London County Council or the Greater London Council.

XXVI	1956	The Parish of St. Mary, Lambeth. Part Two, Southern Area.
XXVII	1957	Spitalfields and Mile End New Town The Parishes of Christ Church and All Saints and the Liberties of Norton Folgate and the Old Artillery Ground
XXVIII	1960	Parish of Hackney. (Part I), Brooke House, a monograph
XXIX, XXX	1960	The Parish of St. James, Westminster, Part One, South of Piccadilly
XXXI, XXXII	1963	The Parish of St. James, Westminster, Part Two, North of Piccadilly

Henceforth the volumes are published for the Greater London Council.

XXXIII, XXXIV	1966	The Parish of St. Anne, Soho.
XXXV	1970	The Theatre Royal, Drury Lane, and The Royal Opera House, Covent Garden
XXXVI	1970	The Parish of St. Paul, Covent Garden
XXXVII	1973	Northern Kensington.
XXXVIII	1975	The Museums Area of South Kensington and Westminster.
XXXIX	1977	The Grosvenor Estate in Mayfair, Part I, General History
XL	1980	The Grosvenor Estate in Mayfair, Part II, The Buildings
XLI	1983	Southern Kensington: Brompton.

Henceforth the General Editor is Hermione Hobhouse.

| XLII | 1986 | Southern Kensington: Kensington Square to Earl's Court. |

Henceforth the volumes are published for the Royal Commission on the Historical Monuments of England.

| XLIII, XLIV | 1994 | Poplar, Blackwall and the Isle of Dogs, the Parish of All Saints, Poplar. |

MONOGRAPH SERIES

Volume	Publication date	Title details
1	1896	The Trinity Hospital in Mile End: An Object Lesson in National History, by C.R. Ashbee, MA, Architect. Being the first monograph of the Committee for the Survey of the Memorials of Greater London.
2	1900	St. Mary Stratford Bow. by Osborn C. Hills, ARIBA with an introductory chapter by C.R. Ashbee, MA, being the second monograph of the Committee for the Survey of the Memorials of Greater London
3	1902	The Old Palace of Bromley-by-Bow. by Ernest Godman, Architect, being the third monograph of the Committee for the Survey of the Memorials of Greater London
4	1903	The Great House, Leyton. by Edwin Gunn, Architect. Being the fourth monograph of the Committee for the Survey of the Memorials of Greater London
5	1904	Brooke House, Hackney. by Ernest A. Mann, Architect. Being the fifth monograph of the Committee for the Survey of the Memorials of Greater London
6	1905	The Church of St. Dunstan, Stepney. by the Hon. W. Pepys and Ernest Godman. Being the sixth monograph of the Committee for the Survey of the Memorials of Greater London
7	1921	East Acton Manor House being the seventh monograph of the London Survey Committee [no author]
8	1907	Sandford Manor, Fulham. by W. Arthur Webb, Architect. Being the eighth monograph of the Committee for the Survey of the Memorials of Greater London
9	1908	Crosby Place. by Philip Norman, FSA, LLD, with an Architectural Description by W.D. Caröe, FSA Being the ninth monograph of the Committee for the Survey of the Memorials of Greater London
10	1916	Morden College, Blackheath, being the tenth monograph of the London Survey Committee by Frank T. Green, ARIBA, PASI.
11	1917	Eastbury Manor House, Barking, being the eleventh monograph of the London Survey Committee, with Drawings by Hubert V.C. Curtis.
12	1926	Cromwell House, Highgate, being the twelfth monograph of the London Survey Committee by Philip Norman, FSA, LLD.
13	1933	Swakeleys, Ickenham, being the thirteenth monograph of the London Survey Committee by Walter H. Godfrey, FSA.
14	1937	The Queen's House, Greenwich, being the fourteenth monograph of the London Survey Committee by George H. Chettle
15	1944	The Church of St. Bride, Fleet St, by Walter H. Godfrey, FSA, Architect, being the fifteenth monograph of the London Survey Committee and the thirty-fifth publication of the Survey of London
16	1963	The College of Arms, Queen Victoria Street, being the sixteenth and final monograph of the London Survey Committee, by Walter H. Godfrey CBE, FSA, FRIBA, assisted by Sir Anthony Wagner, KCVO, D LITT, FSA, Garter King of Arms.
17	1991	County Hall, General Editor, Hermione Hobhouse

Appendix 2 Content and format of the parish surveys

This paper was prepared by the London Survey Committee and agreed at the Joint Publishing Committee with those responsible for the London County Council volumes. It gives an outline for the matter researched and recorded in the volumes.

RESOLVED at a Meeting of the LONDON SURVEY COMMITTEE, 27, Abingdon Street, London, S.W., on April 27th, 1914, that the following Detailed Instructions as to the Content and Format of the Parish Surveys (embodying the practice of the Committee) be submitted to the Publishing Committee of the London County Council for the guidance of the future volumes of the Survey:

I. Content of the Survey

1. Area
The Survey of London to proceed by civil parishes in accordance with the boundaries existing in the year 1894. The recognized unit of each volume to be one civil parish, but this is not to preclude the allocation of more than one volume to a parish where found necessary; or more than one parish to a volume within the area of the City. If it is found desirable for any reason to overstep the parish boundary, any buildings so included are to be repeated in the volume dealing with the adjoining parish to which they belong.

2. Schedule (or Register)
The essential work of the Survey to be the inclusion of every building and object of art or craftsmanship having a permanent position in the parish and dating from a period before the year 1800. Objects not originally in the parish but introduced there permanently to be included in the Survey. Objects of aesthetic interest, and important buildings erected subsequently to 1800 to be included only by special resolution of the Publishing Committee.

3. Graphic Records
All objects included in the schedule which are deemed of sufficient historical, architectural, or aesthetic interest to be amply illustrated by photographs, sketches, measured drawings and details in accordance with the conditions set forth hereinafter. Old prints and drawings should be reproduced to illustrate their former condition, if required.

4. Historical and descriptive notes
The schedule of buildings and other objects, duly numbered for reference, to have attached the following items of information whenever possible:
- (a) Names of ground landlord, leaseholders, etc.
- (b) Condition of repair.
- (c) Description and date of fabric, including a resumé of its historical development, and full details of its various parts and fittings in accordance with the skeleton list hereunder.
- (d) Historical and biographical notes regarding former possessors, occupants, donors, or other persons associated with the buildings or objects described.

NOTE: Under (d) should be included lists of tenants of houses (compiled from the ratebooks, etc.), incumbents of churches, heads of religious or semi-religious houses, etc., etc.

5. General History of the Parish
A separate introduction can be arranged to deal with the General History of the Parish; notes on the development of isolated buildings, roads, streets, etc., being included under (c) and (d) wherever desirable. This section to be fully illustrated by maps and plans.

6. Demolished Buildings
Buildings and objects of interest dating from before 1800, but destroyed and removed from the Parish subsequent to the year 1894 (the date of the commencement of the Survey) can be included if sufficient records exist. Buildings demolished or removed before 1894 to be included only by resolution of the publishing committee.

II. Format of the Volumes

1. Size and Material
Each volume to be a quarto of the size of Chelsea Volume I, agreeing in weight, colour and quality of paper with the same volume, and issued with uncut edges.

2. Number of Pages
It is desirable that no volume exceed three hundred and fifty (350) pages complete.

3. Binding
Each volume to be issued in brown paper covers. A slip should be included with each volume with prices of certain standard bindings already in use.

4. Type
The letterpress to conform in every respect to the type used in Chelsea Volume I.

5. Title Pages
Each volume to have two title pages (a) the general title page of the Survey, and (b) the particular title of the volume, in accordance with Volumes III and IV of the Survey.

6. List of the Survey Committee
Each volume to contain the names of the Joint Publishing Committee and a list of the Honorary and Active members of the Survey Committee, the names of those who have co-operated in the work of a given parish to be marked by an asterisk.

7. Letterpress
The schedule and description of the buildings and objects included in the Survey to be arranged in numerical order, and under the following sub-titles:

1. Ground landlord, leaseholders, etc.
2. Condition of repair.
3. Description and date of fabric.
4. Historical and Biographical notes.
5. Biographical references.
6. Old prints, drawings, etc.
7. In the Council's M.S. collections are: Nos. 4 to 7 to be in small type and each item in Nos. 6 and 7 which is reproduced in the volume to be marked with an asterisk.

Transcripts of all inscriptions, prior to 1800, on monuments within Churches, in Churchyards, Burial Grounds, in public buildings, or on isolated tablets to be made wherever possible, and a selection to be printed in Roman capitals or script, according to the actual lettering on such monuments.

Ordinary references in the letterpress to be marked by footnotes; biographical references being only noted where there are works already published dealing specially with the object under consideration. A bibliography of works dealing with the parish is desirable.

8. Illustrations
Small line drawings, plans, etc., can be introduced in the text by means of line blocks, the bulk of the illustrations being allocated to the plates at the end of the book.

9. Heraldic Illustrations
A proportion of coats of arms of persons mentioned in the text to be selected for marginal illustration. Where the coat of arms actually occurs on a house or monument within the Survey, it should be selected in preference to others and can be drawn with all its quarterings as shown on such monument. Where this does not occur, the simple coat of the family mentioned should be shown. Coats of arms to be drawn and blazoned in accordance with the published rules drawn up for

the Victoria Counties History and the Royal Commission on Historical Monuments (England): to be drawn with a strong firm line without tinctures.

10. Index
Names of persons to be included in the index with the names of those places and buildings which are outside the parish or are not included in the Register.

11. Plates
The plates constitute the Survey's 'record' work, and should be composed of:
>   (a) Measured drawings and plans.
>   (b) Photographs.
>   (c) Old prints and other views.
>   (d) Maps.

(a) All measured drawings should be prepared in clean, firm lines, generally without shading, and should be reproduced by lithography. The lettering to drawings should be in a plain and legible form of Roman Capitals or Italic script, open or solid.

The name of the actual draughtsman to be added.

(b), (c), and (d) to be reproduced by half tone blocks, or by better process whenever possible.

12. Map of the Parish
With each Volume or set of Volumes dealing with a complete parish there must be issued a reproduction of the Ordnance Survey of the Parish, reduced to a convenient size, with the numbers of all buildings included in the London Survey plainly marked in red thereon.

SCHEDULE of objects to be included in the Survey of buildings

Secular

External elevation including reference to:
- (a)   Number of storeys.
- (b)   Material and treatment of walls.
- (c)   Material and treatment of roofs.
- (d)   Gables.
- (e)   Doors.
- (f)   Windows.
- (g)   Chimney stacks.
- (h)   Rainwater heads, etc.
- (i)   Wrought iron railings and other features in the grounds.

Internal
1.   Ceilings.
2.   Cupboards (fixed).
3.   Doors and overdoors.
4.   Fireplaces and mantelpieces.
5.   Glass.
6.   Paintings.
7.   Panelling.
8.   Parquetry and floors.

9. Plasterwork and internal walls.
10. Roofs and beams (internal).
11. Screens.
12. Tapestries.
13. Miscellanea (e.g., Carving, ironwork, locks, etc.).

Also movables, pictures, plate, etc., wherever belonging to an institution or corporate body.

Ecclesiastical

External Features.

Internal fittings:

1. Altars.
2. Bells.
3. Brackets, for Images.
4. Brasses and indents.
5. Chairs.
6. Chests.
7. Communion tables and rails.
8. Cupboards.
9. Doors (oak, etc.)
10. Easter sepulchre.
11. Font and font cover.
12. Galleries.
13. Glass.
14. Images.
15. Lectern.
16. Libraries.
17. Lockers.
18. Monuments and floor slabs.
19. Niches.
20. Paintings (murals and pictures).
21. Panelling.
22. Piscinea.
23. Plate.
24. Poor box.
25. Pulpit.
26. Recesses.
27. Register.
28. Reredos.
29. Royal Arms.
30. Screens.
31. Seating.
32. Sedilia.
33. Stalls.
34. Stoups (holy water).
35. Tiles.
36. Miscellanea (including clocks, hour-glass stands, rainwater heads, sun dials, etc.).
    N.B. Heraldry to be noted where it occurs.
37. Organs and organ cases.
38. Plate and furniture.

Abbreviations

CSMGL	Committee for the Survey of the Memorials of Greater London
DNB	*Dictionary of National Biography*
GA	Godfrey Archive (Godfrey family)
GLC	Greater London Council
GLRO	Greater London Record Office
HABS	Historic American Buildings Survey
JLS	*Journal of the London Society*
JSA	*Journal of the Society of Antiquaries of London*
LCC	London County Council
LTR	*London Topographical Record*
LTS	London Topographical Society
MoL	Museum of London
NBR	National Buildings Record
NMR	National Monuments Record
NMRC	National Monuments Record Centre
PWL	P W Lovell
RCHME	Royal Commission on the Historical Monuments of England
RIBA	Royal Institute of British Architects
SoL	Survey of London
SPAB	Society for the Protection of Ancient Buildings
WHG	W H Godfrey
WWW	*Who Was Who*

Notes

1 Osbert Lancaster, review of Vol XXXVII, *Northern Kensington* (1973), in *Books and Bookmen*, Oct 1973, p 38.

2 LCC minutes, Report by the Clerk for General Purposes, Town Planning and Establishment Committees, 8 July 1952.

3 T F Reddaway, review of Vol XXVII, *Christ Church and All Saints (Spitalfields and Mile End New Town)* (1957), in *History*.

4 GA, PWL to G Callender, 24 Sept 1936.

5 PWL to L Gomme, 28 Apr 1914; papers supplied to Joint Publishing Committee, 11 May 1914.

6 E W Riley, Report to the LCC Historical Records Committee, 9 Oct 1903.

7 *The Bavarian State Conservation Office* (Bayerisches Landesamt für Denkmalpflege, 1987).

8 Society for Photographing the Relics of Old London, Nos 109–20, Apr 1886.

9 Report of 1st AGM, *City Press*, 4 Feb 1882, repr in LTS Newsletter (May 1994), 7–8; Stephen Marks, 'The London Topographical Society: A Brief Account', *LTR* **24** (1980), 1–10.

10 Philip Norman, Preface to *London Vanished and Vanishing* (1905), p vii.

11 Alan Crawford, *C R Ashbee: Architect, Designer and Romantic Socialist* (1985), 57.

12 See *Bromley-by-Bow* (SoL I, 1900); *The Old Palace of Bromley-by-Bow* (SoL Monograph 3, 1902); H Clifford Smith, *The Panelled Rooms*, i. *The Bromley Room* (2nd edn, 1922).

13 C R Ashbee, *The Old Palace of Bromley-by-Bow*, 9.

14 GLRO A/LSC/1, minutes of meeting, 25 June 1994; Crawford, *Ashbee*, 57–66.

15 GA *passim*; Yates obituary: *JSA* **38** (1958), 298.

16 Ashbee, Introduction, *Bromley-by-Bow*, pp xiii–xv.

17 GLRO A/LSC/1, fo. 10.

18 Crawford, *Ashbee*, 60.

19 GLRO A/LSC/2, meeting, 21 July 1908.

20 Lord Hobhouse, in *Speaker*, quoted in L T Hobhouse and J A Hammond, *Memoir of Lord Hobhouse* (1905), 163.

21 Gomme obituary: *Proceedings of the Society of Antiquaries* (1916), 211–12.

22 *DNB*; *WWW 1912–1920*.

23 Historical Records and Buildings Committee, report, adopted by LCC,17 Dec 1901. *Indications of Houses of Historical Interest in London* were issued in several parts: vol i (tablets 1–33), nd but post-1907; vol ii (tablets 33–59), 1909.

24 LCC Report, *Builder*, 27 Feb 1897, p 202.

25 GLRO A/LSC, Committee for the Survey of the Memorials of Greater London (CSMGL), Third Report, May 1897.

26 GLRO A/LSC/1, 19 Apr 1900.

27 Ashbee, Introduction, *Bromley-by-Bow*, p xiii.

28 GLRO, W H Godfrey, Lecture to London Group, London University, 5 Jan 1954, fo. 4.

29 R Meinertzhagen, *Diary of a Black Sheep* (1964), 38; *WWW 1931–1940*.

30 GLRO A/LSC, CSMGL, report, 1906–7.

31 GA *passim*; London Society Archives, Survey Cashbook.

32 Ashbee, Introduction, *Bromley-by-Bow*, pp xxxv–xxxvi.

33 Norman obituaries: Clapham, in *JSA* **11** (1931), 278; *LTR* (1931), 140–3; also W H Godfrey, 'The London Survey Committee, 1894–1952', *LTR* **21** (1958), 79–82.

34 Lovell obituaries: *JSA* **31** (1951), 252, 255; *Builder*, 16 June 1950, p 817; Godfrey, 'The London Survey Committee, 1894–1952'; *JLS* **306** (Oct 1951), 28–9.

35 GA, Godfrey Memoirs, MS, fos 104, 126; J Summerson, 'W H Godfrey: Obituary', *LTR* **22** (1965), 127–35; *50 Years of the National Buildings Record* (RCHME, 1991).

36 W H Godfrey, *Our Building Inheritance* (1944), 23.

37 *Daily Graphic*, 14 July 1907, quoted in W Emil Godfrey, 'Crosby Hall and its Re-erection', *Transactions of the Ancient Monuments Society* NS **26** (1982), 227–43.

38 P Norman, *Crosby Place* (SoL Monograph 9, 1908); W H Godfrey, 'The London Survey Committee, 1894–1952', 85; W Emil Godfrey, 'Crosby Hall and its Re-erection'; A Saint, 'Ashbee, Geddes, Lethaby and the Rebuilding of Crosby Hall', *Architectural History* **34** (1991), 206–25.

39 Saint, 'Ashbee, Geddes, Lethaby and the Rebuilding of Crosby Hall', 208.

40 Crawford, *Ashbee*, 217.

41 'Survey of London', Report by the Architect to the Historical Records Committee, 9 Oct 1903.

42 Godfrey Memoirs, MS, fo. 157.

43 Laurence Gomme, Preface, *Lincoln's Inn Fields (St. Giles-in-the-Fields. Part I)* (SoL III, 1912).

44 Memo of Agreement between the (53) members of the Active Committee and the LCC, 25 July 1910; GLRO A/LSC/2, Minute Book of London Survey Committee, 1907–12.

45 LCC minutes, Report of the Establishment Committee, item 1, 22 Oct 1935, p 301.

46 Fincham obituary: *JSA* **33** (1953), 273.

47 *WWW 1961–1970*.

48 GA, PWL circular letter, 18 Apr 1934. A Centenary Watch Night Party was held on 12 May 1994 at Old Battersea House.

49 Lovell, *JLS* **1** (Oct 1913), 16.

50 GLRO A/LSC, CSMGL, report, 1902.

51 GA, PWL to WHG, 2 Dec 1938.

52 GA, PWL to WHG, 13 Feb 1932.

53 GA, PWL to WHG, 25 Jan 1935.

54 London Society Committee minutes, 1931, *passim*; *JLS* (Sept 1948), 33–4.

55 GA, PWL to D Matheson, 14 Apr 1937; see also PWL to WHG, 18 Jan 1938.

56 GA, Active Committee, minutes, 16 Nov 1936, 18 Oct 1937, 25 Apr 1938, 16 May 1938; PWL to WHG, postcard, 18 Jan 1938.

57 LCC minutes, Report of Local Government Committee, 10 May 1927, p 710.

58 GA, PWL to WHG, 22 Apr 1926.

59 GA, PWL to WHG, 19 Feb 1928; the drawings were made by J M Sheppard FRIBA, of 38 Bedford Place, architect of the new buildings at Berkhamsted. The volume appeared as R H Nichols and F A Wray, *History of the Foundling Hospital* (1935). Some materials from the original buildings were salvaged and are in the hospital's new headquarters at Mecklenburgh Square. For Reginald Hugh Nichols JP FSA, see *JSA* **33** (1953), 272.

60 GA, G Chettle to WHG, 15 Nov 1933; Crawford, *Ashbee*, 445 n 33.

61 *DNB*; *WWW 1951–1960*.

62 GA, PWL to G Callender, 24 Sept 1936. Geoffrey Callender (1875–1946), first Director of the newly formed Maritime Museum, succeeded Meinertzhagen as Hon Treasurer.

63 W H Godfrey, *Swakeleys, Ickenham* (SoL Monograph 13, 1933), p xi.

64 Drawings at the NMRC, credited to London Society, NMR 1947/274–85.

65 For a list of publications by W H Godfrey, see the list by M Honeybourne, *LTR* **22** (1965), 135.

66 Darlington obituary: Marie Draper, *Journal of the Society of Archivists* 4/2 (Oct 1970), 166–8.

67 GA, PWL to WHG, 23 Aug 1935.

68 Dorling obituary: *JSA* **24** (1944), 71.

69 W H Godfrey, Introduction, *Chelsea. Part I* (SoL II, 1909), p xvi.

70 Gomme to members of Joint Publishing Committee, 5 May 1914, enclosing draft. Final version approved by the Committee on 22 June 1914.

71 Introduction, *St. Leonard, Shoreditch* (SoL VIII, 1922), p xv.

72 Honeybourne obituary: *LTR* **24** (1980), 203–10.

73 Jeffries Davis obituary: *JSA* **24** (1944), 177.

74 GA, EJD to WHG, 28 July 1938; PWL to WHG, 3 Nov 1938.

75 Prefaces, *South Bank and Vauxhall (St. Mary, Lambeth. Part I)* (SoL XXIII, 1951), and *St. George's Fields (St. George the Martyr and St. Mary Newington, Southwark)* (SoL XXV, 1955).

76 London Society Committee minutes, 1 Oct 1914.

77 Ashbee Diary, 1915, provided by Alan Crawford.

78 GA, PWL to WHG, 25 Jan 1927.

79 *JLS* **167** (1932), 4.

80 *JLS* **169** (1932), 36.

81 GA, PWL to WHG, 1 Feb 1932.

82 GA, PWL to WHG, 12 Jan 1932.

83 NMRC NBR 1947/129–466.

84 NMRC NBR 1949/45–178, listed as 'London Survey'.

85 NMRC NBR 1951/25–34.

86 GA, PWL to WHG, 25 Jan 1935.

87 GA, PWL to WHG, 22 Jan 1935.

88 GA, PWL to WHG, 25 Jan 1935.

89 GA, PWL to WHG, nd.

90 GA, WHG to E P Wheeler, at his home in Sutton, 24 Aug 1935.

91 GA *passim*, including paper 'My Own Ideas for the Conduct of the Survey'.

92 GA, PWL to WHG, 18 Feb 1938.

93 GA, PWL to WHG, 31 July 1939.

94 GA, PWL to WHG, 31 Aug 1939.

95 GA, telegram, 16 Sept 1939.

96 GLRO, W H Godfrey, Lecture to London Group, London University, 5 Jan 1954, fo. 7.

97 W H Godfrey, draft report, 'London Survey Committee 1894–1944'.

98 Bloe obituary: *JSA* **46** (1966), 394.

99 W H Godfrey, Preface, *St. Pancras. Part III (Tottenham Court Road)* (SoL XXI, 1949), p xix.

100 Phillips obituary: *JSA* **52** (1972).

101 LCC minutes, Report by the Clerk for General Purposes, Town Planning and Establishment Committees, 8 July 1952.

102 W H Godfrey, 'The London Survey Committee', 1894–1952', *LTR* **21** (1958), 91.

103 Marks, 'The London Topographical Society: A Brief Account'.

104 *County Hall* (SoL Monograph 17, 1991), 82.

105 Darlington obituary: Marie Draper, *Journal of the Society of Archivists* 4/2 (Oct 1970), 166–8.

106 Hansard, 22 Jan 1985, Local Government Bill, Standing Committee G, Ground, col 521.

107 Ibid, Leigh, col 522.

108 Preface, *St. Mary, Lambeth. Part II, Southern Area* (SoL XXVI, 1956), pp v–vi.

109 J Summerson, Foreword to H J Dyos, *Victorian Suburb* (1961), 10.

110 *London Journal* 12/1 (summer 1986): *London Survey'd: Essays in Honour of F H W Sheppard*. Marion Ball worked on Vol XXVII, Marie Draper on Vols XXVI–XXXVI, Peter Bezodis on Vols XXVII–XLIII, John Greenacombe on Vols XXXV onwards, Victor Belcher on Vols XXXVI–XLII. Contributions were made by other writers, mostly on architectural descriptions.

111 F H W Sheppard, 'Sources and Methods Used for the Survey of London', in H J Dyos, *The Study of Urban History* (1968), 131–45.

112 Hansard, 22 Jan 1985, cols 540–1. Kenneth Baker refers, incorrectly, to the Royal Commission for Historical Manuscripts.

113 Godfrey Memoirs, MS, fo. 165.

114 Hansard, 22 Jan 1985, Baker, col 541.

Index

Illustration numbers are in **bold** at the end of entries
n refers to an entry in the Notes

The Survey of London – one hundred years old in 1994 – traces its origins to the campaigning zeal of the 1890s when C R Ashbee and a group of like-minded conservationists set up the Watch Committee to campaign against the demolition of historic buildings, such as the Trinity Hospital (1695) in Mile End Road. Out of this grew 'the great enterprise' as Osbert Lancaster described it, of creating an inventory of all London's historic buildings as an aid to their protection. That massive undertaking is still continuing and this book traces the vicissitudes of the Survey over the last hundred years, painting a portrait of an organisation that has often been in the forefront of the conservation movement and whose work has been hailed as 'the London conservationist's Bible'.

ROYAL
COMMISSION
ON THE
HISTORICAL
MONUMENTS
OF ENGLAND

Price **£7.95** net

Front cover: Wych Street, the Strand, in 1901, painted by Philip Norman
Back cover: No. 72 Oxford Gardens: plans, elevations and decorative details

ISBN 1-87359-219-1

9 781873 592199

National Trust

Hindhead Common and the Devil's Punch Bowl

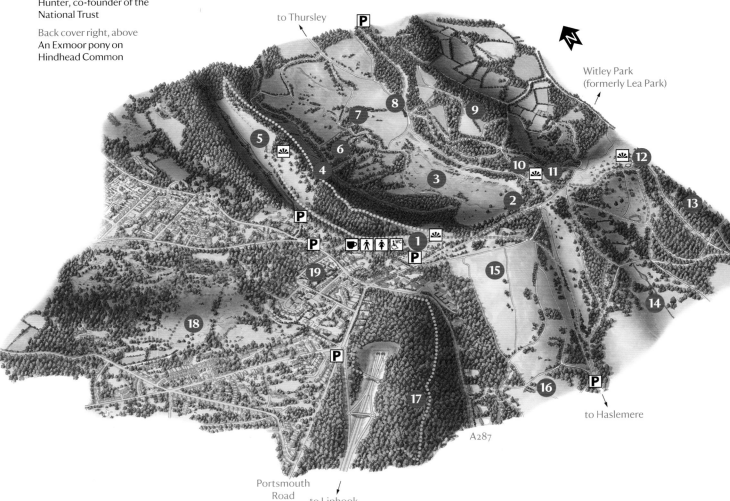

Front cover A view over Sugar Loaf Hill, part of the Devil's Punch Bowl

Opposite A family plays at the Punch Bowl

Back cover left Sir Robert Hunter, co-founder of the National Trust

Back cover right, above An Exmoor pony on Hindhead Common

Back cover right, below Ludshott Common in Autumn

Back cover, central The Sailor's Stone in snow

- Highcombe Hike 2.8 miles (4.5 km)
- Hidden Hindhead 3.1 miles (5 km)
- Sailor's Stroll 1 mile (1.6 km)
- The Golden Valley Walk 2 miles (3.2 km)
- Miss James' Walk 1.9 miles (3 km)

to Thursley

Witley Park (formerly Lea Park)

to Haslemere

to Liphook

Portsmouth Road

A287

Key:
 Car park
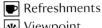 WC
Accessible WC
Refreshments
Viewpoint

1 National Trust Café
2 Sailor's Stone
3 Devil's Punch Bowl
4 Highcombe Edge
5 Robertson Memorial
6 Youth Hostel
7 Gnome Cottage
8 Sugar Loaf Hill
9 Boundless Copse
10 Celtic Cross
11 Gibbet Hill
12 Temple of the Four Winds
13 Hurt Hill
14 Combeswell
15 Hindhead Common
16 Frydinghurst
17 Tyndall's Wood
18 Golden Valley
19 Hindhead